Data Warehousing Advice for Managers

Data Warehousing Advice for Managers

PATRICIA L. FERDINANDI

AMACOM

American Management Association

New York • Atlanta • Boston • Chicago • Kansas City • San Francisco • Washington, D.C.
• Brussels • Mexico City • Tokyo • Toronto

Ferdinandi, Patricia L.
    Data warehousing advice for managers / Patricia L. Ferdinandi.
             p.   cm.
    Includes bibliographical references and index.
    ISBN 0-8144-0409-x
    1. Data warehousing   I. Title.
QA76.9.D37F47   1999
    658.4'038'0285574—dc21   98–28708
                                          CIP

Printing number

10 9 8 7 6 5 4 3 2 1

This book is dedicated to my husband,
Giuseppe, for his loving support

Contents

Acknowledgments

You may be considered an expert on a particular topic. You may have participated in a project that developed a product using a particular technology. You may have consulted multiple organizations about building and using this technology. You may even have had the opportunity to teach others about how to implement this technology. However, nothing is as challenging as writing about a topic on which you are considered knowledgeable. This is especially true when you are writing about a topic like data warehousing, whose technology is changing as rapidly as the words fall on a piece of paper.

When writing a book, you have to write to an audience from whom you do not receive any direct feedback. Your explanations must be clear and concise so that the reader knows exactly what you are trying to convey. Writing a book is one of the most stressful, time-consuming, and rewarding efforts that I have ever undertaken. It forces you to define your approach to the topic in such precise terms that no one can misinterpret the information that you are providing.

I could never have accomplished this milestone without the support of my family, friends, and coworkers. All of the individuals range from minimal to expert level in technological or business knowledge in the area of data warehousing. All provided valuable information as far as content, approach, and moral support. The following people deserve special mention:

> My husband, Giuseppe, for his constant encouragement and attention to detail

> My mother, Louise Smith; sister, Karen; and nieces, Ellen D'Onofrio and Tracy Glock, for their continual "Why aren't you writing"

> My closest and dearest friend, Susan E. Pirog, for her constant enthusiasm

Kassy Cassidy and Irene Voce for their business and reviewing ability

Rebecca Moeller, for her technical sounding board

My editors, Anthony Vlamis, Ray O'Connell, Mike Sivilli, and their staff for their continual guidance and keeping it all together

Maureen Sullivan and Sharon Woleben for their market research and financial "business manager" background

Burt Rosner for his contributions

Platinum Solutions/LBMS for their use of the data warehouse process template

The Data Warehousing Institute for ensuring the quality and ethics of data warehousing professionals

Special thanks to Michael Rothstein, the mentor and guide throughout this process who has had the persistence of authoring several of his own books and a software product

Preface

Target Readers

People are a corporation's strength. Data is the blood of an organization. Without data, the corporation has no idea where it stands and where it will go. Without quick access to quality data, people can not excel at their jobs. With inconsistent or missing data, corporations make incorrect strategic decisions about products, services, and organizations. Any delay in obtaining quality data may result in loosing a competitive advantage. Both of these situations create a bottleneck in a corporation's path to success. Implementing a data warehouse can solve both these situations. A data warehouse is an invaluable strategic tool that facilitates corporate survival and success.

The success of the corporation is dependent upon the success of the data warehouse, which is built based upon business needs, policies, procedures, rules, and strategy. All can be defined by the business manager. Therefore, it is imperative that the business manager understands the basics about data warehousing to ensure its success in meeting the corporation's needs.

Data Warehousing Advice for Managers is written for the business manager who holds a lower- to executive-level management position in any size business organization. However, this organizational title is used loosely. This book is for anyone who is interested in data warehousing, its potential, and guidelines for implementing one. This list includes any administrative, marketing, sales, or financial manager who benefits from reading this book. This book is for any business representative who needs to produce intelligent and sophisticated reports from a large amount of data that is scattered among a number of different data sources.

This book is a survival guide for any noninformation technology manager who needs a complete and consistent source of information. No matter what the business manager's level of computer expertise is, this book will explain the following:

- What a data warehouse is

- How to determine if the company needs one

- How to build one successfully

- What to do with it once the company has one

- How to sell the need to management

All of which are for the sole purpose of successfully implementing a data warehouse to further the success of the corporation.

This book's target reader probably holds one of the following positions:

Business representative. This is a generic name for anyone from a noninformation systems organization who participates in the development and implementation effort. This person can range from a corporate executive down to a data entry clerk. This individual works for any organization, company, or group that has a great deal of data but is unable to access it and manipulate it to produce meaningful information. From the general concept to the detailed deliverables, the business representative needs minimal or no previous interaction with developing a data warehouse system or any computer system to benefit from reading this book.

Business executive. Building a data warehouse is costly and risky. Therefore, involving executive support in the process helps software developers align what information to contain in the data warehouse with the company's goals. Regular executive participation prevents information requirements from being unduly influenced by one particular business division or becoming bogged down in organizational rivalries. No matter what size data warehouse is to be implemented, it needs to be aligned with the strategic goals of the corporation. Therefore, the business executive, representing middle to upper management, would gain insight from this book by understanding what a data warehouse is and what it can do for the corporation. After reading this book, the business executive will be able to identify the right business manager to facilitate the effort.

Business manager. The primary audience for this book is the business representative who initiates the request and who is responsible for the payment and coordination of the data warehouse. The other alternative is that the business manager is put in charge by the business executive to deliver an effective data warehouse. As a result, the business manager will spend many hours working with the information technology group and will have the authority to commit other business resources. It does not matter if the person has never interacted with the information technology department before. This book will educate the business manager about the subject of data warehousing so that he or she will be able to clearly define the requirements and understand the costs with confidence.

Business knowledge expert.[1] One of the committed resources needs to be a business representative who has detailed knowledge of the business that the data warehouse will satisfy. It will be up to the business knowledge expert to explicitly convey the details for all or part of the contents of the data warehouse and what the organization of the contents implies. This person will be considered the knowledge expert because he or she will provide detailed information about the definition and uses of pertinent corporate information for all or specific areas of interest, such as marketing, sales, or human resources. Many business knowledge experts participate in the design, development, and implementation of the data warehouse. It is up to the business manager to control and coordinate their involvement.

Business analyst. The primary users of a data warehouse are the analysts who are responsible for market research, statistical analysis, or any type of trend "what-if" analysis. These business representatives can gain insight from this book by learning about a data warehouse and its capabilities. These business representatives may take on the role of "knowledge experts" during the design or implementation of the data warehouse. Even if they do not, the business analyst will be more productive in using the data warehouse because he or she understands the basic concepts reviewed in this book.

Business liaison. In many organizations, there is a person who inter-faces with the business community and the information technology group. The business liaison could be either a person from the business community or the information technology group. In either case, one of the roles of the business liaison may be to explain the benefits or the process of implementing a data warehouse in business terms. The business liaison can benefit from reading this book, which will help translate the technological terms and processes into something understandable to the business representative participants.

Data Warehousing Advice for Managers is written for the business community. However, information technology managers will find this book to be a valuable tool for understanding where common communication has previously failed between the business organization and information technologists. This book will enlighten the information technology professional about how the business manager will use a data warehouse and how to describe its benefits to his or her business. A data warehouse can not be designed, developed, or implemented solely with information technologists. It requires the efforts of the business community as well. It will behoove the information technologist to read this book to facilitate the communication between business and his or her group.

Because of the rapid pace at which the global market operates, it is important to take advantage of any strategic tool that gives the corporation a competitive advantage. With the involvement of the business manager, a data warehouse can be successfully implemented to provide that competitive advantage.

Data Warehousing
Advice for Managers

1

Data Warehousing

C ongratulations! You are about to embark on a journey to obtain knowledge about a strategic tool for your corporate survival . . . data warehousing. You are a business manager who needs timely, accurate data that can be analyzed in multiple formats to identify new business opportunities. You have learned that a technological solution called data warehousing exists, but you need to learn more about it to take advantage of its potential. Common questions often arise when interpreting a technological solution such as a data warehousing. Such questions include:

- What is it?
- What will it do for me?
- How much does it cost?
- What are the risks associated with its implementation?
- How can I control the effort?
- How are my competitors taking advantage of data warehousing?
- What other tools are available to help me with my analysis?
- Will a data warehouse provide accurate information that improves competition in today's global marketplace?

All of these issues are discussed in this book. However, a little background information will enable the business manager to interpret the what, where, when, how, why of data warehousing and its related technologies.

Background

Data and people are at the heart of corporate survival. People are the most important asset to any corporation. However people, and thus the corporation, are put at a disadvantage without good quality, timely data. In the typical corporate scenario, people are doing their jobs and making crucial decisions with inconsistent, invalid, or missing data. Bottlenecks are inherent to the process because of delayed delivery, manual manipulation, and follow-up verification of crucial decision-making data.

Data is needed to define and continually reassess corporate strategy and direction. It is needed to determine an organization's health. Data illustrates a corporation's market share effectiveness. Data is used to develop new products and services, to forecast and review past results. Data is used to predict the impact of organizational changes, employee strikes, or customer trends. Data is required to back up advertising concepts or legal claims.

If data is crucial for a corporation to function, and people are its most valuable resource, then why does your corporation operate without providing valid data to its employees?

Business managers acknowledge that competitiveness in today's global marketplace is increasingly dependent on the scope and timeliness of data, and on the productivity of knowledge workers. In order to maintain a competitive advantage, information must be quickly delivered in a manner that can be easily understood and manipulated. Therefore, it is imperative for a corporation's growth and success that information technology provides access and analytical facilities for more information.

Many technologies currently exist that assist businesses in obtaining a competitive advantage. One of the primary technologies that is on every businessperson's mind is the Internet.[1] The Internet is an extremely important communication mechanism that provides information. The Internet provides increased access to information for a corporation and provides a communication facility to reach a wider audience.[2]

The key words in the above paragraph are *access* and *communication* of information. The Internet is not the information or the data that provides information. It is not the storage of data. It is not the completeness or consistency of data. In order to be complete, consistent, and accessible in a timely manner, data must be kept in a well-designed data warehouse.

The purpose of a data warehouse is to store clear, concise, and consistent data in a format that can be easily and quickly accessed by the business community. It is the automated filing cabinet of all data required by a corporation. The difference between a data warehouse and other data storage facilities is that the data is organized specifically for analytical analysis. The data is organized in a format that easily answers questions from the business community. It contains data that may provide the competitive advantage required in a global economy. Data is stored in a framework to provide the quickest access by targeted business users who are either internal or external to the corporation. Again, this data sits until a businessperson requires it.

What This Book Is All About

It takes a great deal of effort to plan, design, develop, and implement a data warehouse. The time and cost involved must be evaluated against the potential business benefits of having data immediately available to key decision makers. If the process is managed properly, the benefits will outweigh the time and costs.

The purpose of *Data Warehousing Advice for Managers* is to assist readers in determining the value of implementing data warehouses in their organizations.

Although building a data warehouse can be costly and time consuming, it may be necessary for your corporation to do so to remain competitive. The key is to identify the benefits and manage the implementation. The process must be managed indirectly by the business manager to reduce cost and time without sacrificing quality. To determine if a data warehouse is crucial for a corporation's survival, this book will explain to the business manager:

1. What a data warehouse is and how it can be used

2. How to ensure that implementation is successful and how to obtain the highest return on investment (ROI)

3. How to coordinate a data warehouse with other technologies

4. How to convince executive management that the corporation must have one to be competitive, especially during this cost-conscious era

5. How to find out where to obtain more information and training

The business manager reading this book:

- May be a novice when it comes to computers
- May be a power user
- May be completely frustrated by previous or current involvement with information system development

By understanding the basic concepts of a data warehouse, the business manager:

- Will be able to convey his or her data and usage requirements
- Will be able to understand the potential a data warehouse can provide the corporation
- Will be able to indirectly manage the project to ensure its compliance with requirements

This book introduces business managers to the best practices for implementing a data warehouse. After reading this book, a business manager will be able to determine what can be achieved with this pool of data. It will enable the business manager, in combination with his or her business knowledge, to create a smooth transition among the strategic direction, idea, request, development, and ultimate delivery of a quality data warehouse that positively impacts on the corporation's bottom line.

This is not a detailed book that will enable a business manager to directly manage or do the effort. However, it will provide enough information for the business manager to know if, and ensure that, the corporation will obtain maximum benefit from implementing a data warehouse. This book does not use a technical approach to the material, but rather a tactical business approach. The business manager will receive enough information to determine and document a data warehouse's value to the corporation. He or she will understand the business implications of implementing a well-designed data warehouse and the key strategies needed to ensure its success.

The ultimate goal is to achieve positive business results using information technology. A business manager's efforts are better spent running the business. However, business managers also need to understand the

limits of what a data warehouse can do for the corporation to use it efficiently. Therefore, several sections of this book are dedicated to discussing
what to do and not do with a data warehouse and the implementation
process.

Book Organization

This chapter explains the basic concepts of data warehousing. A data
warehouse is a strategic tool that can satisfy some of a corporation's business requirements. This is accomplished:

- With a discussion of what a data warehouse is

- By reviewing the most common benefits to the corporation

- With a realization of what the competition is doing with this technology

- By taking a brief look into the future of data warehousing

Chapter 2, "How a Data Warehouse Is Built," provides an overview of
the process of designing, building, and implementing a data warehouse.
With this knowledge, a business manager will be able to maintain control
of the effort and clearly see how his or her business knowledge will facilitate the effort. With his or her managerial experience, the business manager will understand how to control the effort to ensure that the needs of
the business are satisfied.

Building and implementing a data warehouse is both expensive and
resource intensive. To ensure the optimal use of both finances and
resources, Chapter 3, "Keys to a Successful Implementation," reviews the
most common pitfalls to avoid and processes to put in place to ensure
success. Chapter 3 will teach valuable techniques for implementing a
data warehouse to produce maximum return on investment (ROI). Many
of the topics discussed will benefit business managers working on any
type of information technology project. However, the primary focus and
examples are on implementing a quality data warehouse in a timely manner that will satisfy business information requirements.

Once the reader has an idea of *what* to implement, the question
always asked is what to do with it. Chapter 4, "What Do I Do With It Now?"
reviews some of the endless opportunities a data warehouse can provide
when merged with other technologies. Discussion topics include hot
technology topics such as the Internet or Electronic Data Interchange,

data mining,[3] and other common technologies currently available and used in conjunction with data warehouses.

The first four chapters confirmed your suspicion that data warehouses are needed by corporations to meet today's ever changing competitive challenges. Chapter 5, "How to Prepare a Winning Business Case," guides the readers in initiating the process in their organizations. This chapter reviews the specific benefits and costs of implementing a data warehouse that executive management will want to know before approving the project. Chapter 5 assists the reader with sample forms to use and formulas to determine time, cost, and, most importantly, ROI.

Chapter 6, "Selling a Winning Business Case," assembles all the information gathered from following the steps outlined in Chapter 5 into a format for executive management's approval.

Although this book introduces and comprehensively interprets the technological concepts of data warehousing, more detailed information is available from other sources. Chapter 7, "What to Do About Employee Training and Education," identifies key sources for more in-depth information, including publications, training courses, web sites, and companies that specialize in building or providing products for data warehouses. Chapter 7 lists a subset of available sources on data warehousing. Since the list grows daily, Chapter 7 provides avenues to research for new information. The items listed are for the next level of detail that a business manager may want to pursue.

Information technology is the number one source of acronyms and mnemonics that resemble alphabet soup. This is especially true when the same mnemonics are used to mean totally different things. It is easy to become lost or confused. Therefore, one section is dedicated to explaining the most common terms used for data warehouses. The Technophobia Avoidance Glossary is a convenient reference when reading about data warehousing or discussing it with anyone (especially information technologists). The glossary terms will assist the reader when encountering other material on data warehousing that might otherwise prevent full interpretation and understanding of the material.

What This Chapter Covers

The purpose of Chapter 1 is to introduce business managers to the basic concepts of data warehousing so that they can determine whether or not a data warehouse is the proper strategic tool to benefit their corporations. Considering the previously stated objectives of this book, readers will be able to determine how data warehousing can improve their current business operations.

This will be accomplished by explaining in detail what a data warehouse is and why it differs from other software development projects. Next, information is provided to help readers determine if their corporation needs a data warehouse. Once a reader decides that he or she needs one, a discussion begins about the benefits of implementing a data warehouse in his or her organization. This discussion provides information that could be used as key tangible benefits when writing a winning business case.[4]

Finally, this chapter provides information about what the competition is doing with data warehousing. In most cases, specific companies are not identified.[5] In these instances, generic uses by industry are presented as additional information. The reader should have a basic idea whether to pursue the effort by understanding:

- What a data warehouse is and its benefits

- What is involved in implementing a data warehouse

- What the competition is doing

Using this information, a business manager can obtain more detail by reading Chapter 2, "How a Data Warehouse is Built," to ensure the data warehouse's success.

Defining a Data Warehouse

A data warehouse is a pool of data organized in a format that enables users to interpret data and convert it into information to gain knowledge from this interpretation. It is a single place[6] that contains complete and consistent data obtained from multiple sources. If planned and designed correctly, it is a single place where all business users can access the pool of data to obtain a consistent answer. Data warehousing is the act of a business representative (analyst or executive) extracting business value from the data stored in the data warehouse. The mechanism to do this is specialized, but user-friendly technical tools that work with the data warehouse are available.

A data warehouse differs from other technological solutions or information systems the business community may have come in contact with in the past. It provides data that can be manipulated by its individual users.

It is an "informational" type system that may not store the results of the manipulation. The data contained in the data warehouse is not typically updated as soon as new information is available. The data is updated according to a predetermined schedule. This schedule can be hourly, daily, weekly, or monthly. It is determined by the needs of the business, the availability of the data, and by the process required to "clean"[7] the data.

Other information systems that the business community comes in contact with are "operational" in nature. These systems provide means of supplying data to be stored and used for transactional purposes. Examples of operational systems are purchase-ordering systems or systems that produce regular output, such as payroll checks and reports. These systems fall into the category of on-line transaction processing (OLTP) systems. They are designed to process a specific set of functions in the shortest amount of time.

A data warehouse falls into the category of on-line analytical processing (OLAP)[8] systems. They are designed to provide the most flexibility in answering to a wide range of ad hoc questions. The key differences between the two types of information systems are *processing specific functions* versus *providing flexibility for undetermined analysis.*

Developing a data warehouse system is different from developing prior information systems because the business environment has changed. Previously, business users were passive recipients of canned reports. When developing a data warehouse, business users become active participants in the total data analysis process. They are in control of what is developed and how it is used.

The purpose of a data warehouse environment is to collect and prepare data for access and delivery. Information is created through the interaction of a business representative that is driven by a business need and question. The data warehouse is the packaging vehicle for this raw data.

Do You Need One?

Any corporation that requires complex analysis of a significant amount of data to remain competitive needs a data warehouse. Within your organization, you are currently attempting to obtain answers from out-dated, corrupted legacy information systems. This process is complex, lengthy, resource-intensive, and frustrating. The business community probably questions the accuracy since it receives different results due to the multiple sources of the information needed.

However, justifying the implementation of a data warehouse solely on the basis that it will resolve current data consistency problems seldom succeeds. The justification for implementing a data warehouse must be tied to the strategic direction of the corporation.

If your corporation requires access to information for analyzing situations and making critical decisions that impact the corporate bottom line, then it requires a data warehouse. A data warehouse is the storage of data that assists a business in making critical decisions in an effective manner. The decisions that need to be made can be market driven for new products or services, or tactically driven such as assessing the impact of moving corporate resources.

Basically, a coporation should invest in a data warehouse to provide a pool of data to the business community that is related to anything that requires quality information to assist at any level of decision making. If your organization is attempting to manage the vast amount of knowledge available to its employees, a data warehouse should be part of the solution. It can store the information that key individuals require to become knowledgeable.[9] By allowing access to the data contained in the data warehouse, you are managing the knowledge at the lowest level. Everyone could have access to the same information and can derive similar knowledge from that information.

If your organization needs a facility to interpret vast amounts of diverse data, invest in a data warehouse. After all, the ability to learn faster than your competitors may be the only sustainable competitive advantage your corporation may have.[10]

The biggest advantage of a data warehouse is having a single source for accurate information.[11] The most time-consuming task involved in implementing a data warehouse is "cleansing" the data. The cleansing process first involves identifying the correct source of each piece of data to be stored in the data warehouse. Next, correct interpretation of the data must be determined. Each department that wants access to the data warehouse may have different interpretations to the definition of the data and its relationship to other pieces of data. To bring this point home, ask different business units to define customer or product.

A data warehouse provides a facility to separate operational data from informational data. Operational data is data gathered from business transactional-oriented information systems. Examples are order-entry, on-line banking, or billing systems. These operational systems require quick processing of high-volume transactions. Inquiry-type requests take a much lower priority when attempting to access operational data. Therefore, a data warehouse could be created from operational data but kept separate from it. The data contained in a data warehouse could be made available in a timely manner without impacting on operational transactions required to run the business.

The benefit of what data to have available depends on corporate strategy. The strategy could be future directions, such as new products or services. The strategy could also be daily or tactical in nature, such as the manipulation of inventory.

If the corporate strategy is to branch into a new line of business, data can be made available to the business community of competitor successes in the similar business. This data can be correlated with demographic information to determine the target consumer. At the same time, the data can be searched to determine the staff cost of breaking into this new business venture.[12]

Given this scenario, the business manager needs to determine the cost of implementing a data warehouse. Does this cost outweigh the time and frustration of the current paper intensive process, the cost of outsourcing to a research vendor, or lost opportunities? The information may not be available through other sources.

A tactical use for a data warehouse is the corporate strategy of using just-in-time inventory. This strategy involves logistically purchasing and moving inventory in the most cost-efficient manner. The data warehouse can contain data that is related to current and historical purchasing patterns along with demographics, storage facilities, costs, and travel routes. This would be an example of a tactical use for a data warehouse that impacts the corporation's bottom line on a daily basis.

Knowledge management[13] is becoming increasingly important as employee turnover increases. Turnover may be caused by downsizing, outsourcing, eliminating the use of consultants, or just the revolving door policy of key employees. The important thing is to not lose all the knowledge that the employee (or consultant) obtained while working at the corporation. A data warehouse can store information that assisted the businessperson in developing the knowledge that is so key to corporate survival. Standard or ad hoc inquiries that manipulate data into specific information that evolved into knowledge can be stored and used by those business managers who replaced the ones that left. A data warehouse is a central source of data that allows increased sharing of a key corporate resource . . . data that provides information that evolves into knowledge.

A data warehouse provides the business community with access to historical data that is hard to access, interpret, or present from the traditional operational data reports. By identifying what data is needed by the business community, you identify the difficulty in obtaining, validating, manipulating the data. Measure that need to time spent and you have begun to determine how a data warehouse could benefit your corporation.

Understanding the benefits and possibilities that a data warehouse could provide for your organization is only part of the equation in determining the ROI. Before committing to the project, it is necessary to understand how a data warehouse is built to understand the underlying costs associated with it.

What Is the Competition Doing?

A data warehouse, when properly designed and implemented, is imperative in today's globally competitive market. Therefore, your competition is probably at some stage of development if they do not already have one in place. Your competition is using its data warehouse as an essential weapon against your company. The business strategy of your competition's data warehouse may be the same as yours:

- To increase revenues

- To increase market share

- To reduce costs and expenses

Different corporations implement data warehouses in different ways. Many do not disclose their exact uses because of competitive reasons. Therefore, this section will discuss in general terms what specific industries are accomplishing or plan to accomplish with their data warehouses. Each industry will correlate the possible analysis a data warehouse can provide to the business's core. For the industry that best suits your corporation, imagine your department's main purpose, and determine how you may want to see information pertaining to that purpose. Do not limit yourself to a two-dimensional (spreadsheet) array. Think in terms of a cube and how you may wish to see information either graphically or in tabular form, with a three-(or more) dimensional view. Identify the time slices in which you want to view summarized information or detail (for example, daily, weekly, or quarterly).

Trends over the next couple of years will involve anything related to the Year 2000 and European currency issues. Information will be required to identify the impact of both of these issues. Corporations are combining data warehouses with other tools, such as data mining,[14] for statistical analytical analysis to identify the business risk of noncompliance.

Corporations that already have some type of data warehouse are using the data contained in them to determine impact on the following:

- Market share fluctuations

- Adjustments to policy and procedures

- Changes in resources

According to the META Group,[15] a leading research organization, "customer-centricity" will create 100 percent growth in business areas such as customer service, sales, and marketing. One of the information technology enablers will be the implementation of data warehouses.[16]

One of the dimensions for all research using a data warehouse is velocity. Howard Rubin illustrates the importance of this dimension in many of his presentations and papers. It is not important when a corporation reachs its business objectives but when its competition reaches that point. Think of a highway. You want to drive from Maine to Florida. You take Route 95 and are driving fifty-five miles-per-hour. You will reach your goal. However, your competition is driving at seventy-five miles-per-hour from the same point to reach the same destination. Data warehousing will assist you in either interpreting the speed of the competition or provide data to users at a velocity required to beat the competition.

Figure 1-1 is a generic summary of how different industries initially use data warehouses. The more advanced customers use different-size data warehouses to accomplish all facets of their business. For simplicity, the uses of data warehouses are grouped into the following categories:

- *Product/Service Development* applies to using data to determine which products and services to develop as well as determining the profitability of each product and service.

- *Operations Process Improvement* applies to using data to determine how the manufacturing process can be improved using cost-containment analysis.

Figure 1-1. Industry data warehouse uses.

	PRODUCT/ SERVICE DEVELOPMENT	OPERATIONS/ PROCESS IMPROVEMENT	LOGISTICS/ DISTRIBUTION	MARKETING	ORGANIZATIONAL DEVELOPMENT
ENTERTAINMENT	X			X	
FINANCIAL	X			X	X
GOVERNMENT		X	X		X
MANUFACTURING	X	X			
HEALTHCARE/ MEDICAL/ PHARMACEUTICAL	X	X			
PUBLISHING	X			X	
RETAIL	X		X	X	
TRANSPORTATION	X	X	X		X
UTILITIES	X			X	

- *Logistics/Distribution* pertains to data about inventory management and determines the most efficient and effective means of going from one point to another.

- *Marketing* pertains to data concerning advertising effectiveness and demographics. Basically, marketing is concerned with predicting customer behavior.

- *Organizational Development* pertains to data about the organization, which includes financial stability, risk assessment, and human resource effectiveness and mobility.

Entertainment

Television and movies are the first type of entertainment that comes to mind. What does the public want to see, read, or hear? Is it different by location? How strong is the need for more family-oriented entertainment? What is the best time slot for advertisers based upon the shows and the desired future customers? How much will customers pay for viewing sporting activities? How many attendees can we expect?

Sporting activities also fall under the entertainment category. IBM recently held a symposium[17] that discussed how using a data warehouse provides access to data assets that contribute to better business decisions. The success story example pertains to the coaches of the National Basketball Association (NBA). They used a data warehouse, combined with related technologies, to analyze past games. By understanding which characteristics influenced a game, they were able to identify improvements for the future. The analysis also included understanding the characteristics of customer loyalty. What influenced them the most?

Financial

For the purposes of this section, the term *financial* includes brokerage, banking, and insurance. Brokerage includes monitoring buying trends and requires a great deal of analysis of a corporation's financial position against national and global economy. Risk and portfolio management require quick reaction to market trends. Brokers and dealers make better decisions with timely data about their risk exposure. Most brokers and dealers currently have to wait until the next morning for hard-copy reports. The reaction to any exposure is delayed for at least twenty-four hours. To determine if their reaction was made correctly would be another delay of twenty-four hours. Data warehousing provides a vehicle for responding to and correcting market changes more swiftly.

Credit cards are another financial product that have many uses for a data warehouse. What customers do you want to target with a new card? Is a new applicant credit worthy? What added services can you provide when you go into a joint venture with another company in a different industry? For example, American Express recently started a frequent point program that can be transferred to assorted airline and hotel programs. If not already in place, a data warehouse would assist them in determining the effect this new service has on increased usage of their card.

The banking industry needs a data warehouse to observe global financial markets. It requires forecasting the exchange rate. The industry must analyze data to determine the impact of European currency, especially with the impact of the European Monetary Unit (EMU). Banking branch locations are important to new customers. Where would the best location be for an Automated Teller System (ATM)? Will customers accept a charge for its usage?

The insurance industry needs to analyze claim histories. A data warehouse could contain claim histories and customer profiles. This information could be used to determine fraudulent claims or to identify potentially accident-prone clients. The government is considering adding restrictions to automobile insurance coverage in some states. What impact will these restrictions have on the current revenue base? Reinsurance, or insurance between insurance companies, is based upon the prediction of risk. A data warehouse of past claim histories and weather predictions can assist in determining the cost and terms of a reinsurance contract.

Government

The government includes both civilian and military branches. Governmental agencies that investigate or implement data warehouses range in functional areas. They have their own research for medicine and science. They are involved in manufacturing and determining causes of defects in a process or product. They are involved in war or foreign affairs strategies. Government agencies use data warehousing for either mission-oriented or management and administration-type research. This use is slightly different from the commercial community, which uses data warehouses to maximize profits in a competitive environment. At a state level, analysis is usually geared toward budgets. State agencies require data to determine what moneys are used where, the impact of expense reduction plans on the budget, the impact of labor negotiations, and how many police or firefighters should be added and how will the cost reduce crime.

Healthcare/Medical/Pharmaceutical

This section discusses the use of data warehouses in hospitals, medical research, and pharmaceutical companies.

Hospitals are interested in disease modeling and patient severity outcomes. They also require data to assist them in negotiating managed care contracts with doctors and insurance companies. This includes:

- What drug combination has been the most effective on each illness by sex, location, season, and age group?

- What other over-the-counter products use a specific chemical?

- Which herbs have facilitated the healing process?

- What common factors have caused the influx of patients into the emergency room?

With the introduction and ever increasing use of health maintenance organizations (HMOs), cost management has been one of the many uses of data warehouses. The business subject areas include financial data, doctor qualifications, and patient information to determine the cost of treating patients and the effectiveness of those treatments. It is used to track and control costs. Does keeping patients in the hospital an extra day for different procedures prevent expensive relapses? Does a generic brand really cost less than a brand name when comparing effectiveness of treatment? What cost-effective process improvements can be made to reduce patient waiting time and overall costs to the hospital?

Manufacturing

The goal of manufacturing is to control production costs. This process requires human resource information as well as production records, and even an analysis of whether or not the use of foreign labor produces a quality product.

Operational data available in a data warehouse could assist engineers and managers to maintain consistent quality. The old saying is that 80 percent of problems are found in 20 percent of the product. Therefore, engineers can identify the 20 percent problem area with pattern recognition tools. The problem might be in the assembly process or in specific part failures. They can redesign and analyze the impact of that redesign quicker with the operational data contained in the data warehouse.

Let us include agriculture under manufacturing. A data warehouse could assist in determining which conditions or factors contributed to crop yield. In this scenario, both good and bad factors that resulted in both good and bad crop yields are important in determining adjustments to the process. The time and cost expenditure of attempting new formulas or processes that had little or no impact on the produced yield could be minimized.

Publishing

The first thing that a person thinks about news reporting (whether it be via television, newspaper, magazines, books, or radio) is what is happening now. At first, it does not seem possible that a data warehouse, with its vast historical data, could assist in reporting current events. However, a great deal of research is required for stories. Having the information faster than the competitor may enhance the chances of being "first" with a breaking story.

Publishing also includes fiction and nonfiction books. Authors need access to a great deal of factual information and trends. Imagine the possibilities if all authors had the ability to access historical data from different sources via the Internet. Imagine being the primary, chargeable source of this information.

Forecasting what readers are interested in is an important aspect of publishing. What articles are readers interested in? Did a specific article affect sales last month? What "hot topics" will be required reading two years from now? Which authors have the experience and writing capability to produce quality work in those areas in a short time frame? Who will be the next Stephen King?

Retail

The retail industry is extremely interested in anything that can analyze consumer trends and interests. Retail includes businesses involved in selling, such as stores, television, radio, or mail-order catalogs. Data contained in data warehouses will help determine "just-in-time" inventory with sufficient replenishment notification. All types of retail companies are applying affinity analysis to point-of-sale data to improve their order-cycling, forecasting, sales-reporting, and customer profiling.

- What impact does a specific advertisement campaign have on specific products or services?

- Did the customer base increase from enhancements made to an existing product or service?

- What is the customer base by region and economic standing?

- Who are the customers and what is their goal in going to specific stores or departments during different times of the year?

- What is selling this week? What will be the continual demand for beanie babies?

- What is the best shelf-space positioning that will increase sales?

- What characteristics should a promotion have to reduce unwanted inventory?

- What is the impact of changing demographics on small family-run businesses?

- What would be the impact to the corporation, by product and customer base, if shipping and handling charges were increased?[18]

Transportation

In addition to the marketing and financial answers, a well-designed data warehouse could provide transportation and basic logistic information. For the purposes of this section, transportation consists of airlines, car rentals, and package delivery companies. Logistics are at the core of the transportation industry's business and require careful planning with information that can be contained in a data warehouse. Some analyses could include:

- *For airlines:* What adjustments in equipment and staff would be required to handle a predicted shift in travel trends? What combination of equipment, location, flight pattern, price, and time slot would fill the airplanes? What adjustments to frequent flyer point systems would increase the customer base?

- *For car rentals:* What are the hottest trends in vacations and should cars be shifted between pickup locations to handle a shift in needs? Can a rise in the type of car rental be predicted using the national unemployment statistics by region?

- *For package delivery:* Which season, by region, has the highest volume? How should routes be adjusted to reflect fluctuations in volume or usage to maintain delivery restrictions? What is the impact of increasing or closing districts due to fluctuation in volume or staff? What would the impact of a new service be on the delivery schedule and route? What was and will be the financial impact of the teamster strike? What financial and service mearsures will bring back customers?

Utilities

The gas and electric companies are about to divest as AT&T did in the 1980s. Planning and analyzing the impact on corporate stability requires a great deal of information. Knowledge and critical decisions could be obtained from the data kept in a data warehouse.

- What is the impact on the corporation after loosing key products and services?

- Which customers will be lost by product and region?

- What changes can be made to lost products to regain the customer base?

Entergy Services[19] acknowledges the deregulation of the power industry. This is a key point in their current business strategy. To prepare, they implemented a data warehouse to fight their competitors for the 2.5 million customers in Arkansas, Louisiana, Mississippi, and Texas. Entergy is using its data warehouse to better understand its energy production and administrative costs. Their data warehouse, along with data mining tools, is assisting them in developing a profile of different types of customers: the potentially dissatisfied ones who will opt for their competitor and potential new customers. The data warehouse provides more in-depth types of information than they previously had to help them develop new services. As a result of implementing a data warehouse at Entergy Services, the company:

> has increased reporting flexibility and reduced report costs, [and created] faster access to critical information and an overall improvement in its ability to analyze complex business issues in order to make better business decisions.[20]

Entergy Services has turned this technological solution into a competitive weapon.

Utilities, for the purpose of this book, include telecommunication industries. AT&T, MCI, and many other telephone companies are competing for customer business with additional products and customized services. Customer segmentation analysis is one reason why many of telecommunication companies are implementing data warehouses. With a data warehouse, an analysis can be performed during and after every promotion to determine its effectiveness. This procedure would reduce the cost of continuing costly promotions and illustrate if there is a need to develop a full-service option.

General Uses

Each industry does have common uses for a data warehouse. These uses involve human resources, corporate stability, and the impact of new products and services. Fluctuation in employment affects workload as well as office space.

- What predicted skill and staff level will accept the voluntary layoff package?

- What type of layoff package do you want to offer to minimize the risk of loosing key individuals?

- Does the cost of moving employees between buildings outweigh the cost of maintaining the building?

- What is the impact of increasing wages for specific roles and titles? Is outsourcing a viable solution?

- What are the key improvements culled from opinion surveys that are needed by division and skill level that will improve morale?

- What will be the predicted ROI for implementing a new product or service?

- What products must be improved, phased out, or discontinued to improve the corporation's bottom line?

- What defects affect product sales?

- How can we reduce the market acceptance period of a new product or service?

- Considering past history, how much time and manpower will it take to implement a new product?

- What characteristics affect the turnover of products?

All these uses are centered around data analysis, which can include:

- Pattern identification

- Relationship discovery

- Descriptive, explanatory, predictive, and prescriptive statistical modeling

The data stored in a data warehouse is not only in statistical format. Multimedia data is being stored along with the character and binary format of the past. Therefore, a piece of data could be a motion picture or an image. These items can also provide knowledge to the business community. It is up to the business community to define what type of information should be captured and stored in its data warehouse.

You should now have a good idea about the possibilities of implementing a data warehouse. A data warehouse is a pool of data organized to provide valuable information to those who require it. Those individuals become knowledgeable by interpreting the information received.

Once the type of information and analysis to be associated with it are determined, you need to identify the mechanism. The competition is combining the power of the data warehouse with the Internet and analytical tools.

As you will read in the following section, building a data warehouse to gain knowledge is not a minor task. It will be up to the business manager to determine the feasibility, the benefits, and the return on investment to the corporation.

Competitive Predictions

The competition does not rely on stand-alone data warehouses. Other technologies are being investigated to merge with data warehousing to obtain maximum potential. The most common is the Internet. Giving external users access to the data warehouse can be a revenue-generating competitive advantage. The business questions surrounding this procedure will be the best way to implement user access, security, and billing details.

In order to survive in a globally competitive market, nonsensitive information will need to be shared among corporations with similar interests. Therefore, Extranets (a type of Intranet) will be combined with data mining (analytical facilities) products to query multiple data warehouses.[21] This merger will reduce costs while providing access to a wider range of required information. The World Wide Web is a natural tool for data warehousing because it:

- Is less expensive.

- Provides a universal interface.

- Requires less administrative overhead.

- Provides portable code across technological platforms.

This procedure will require careful planning to avoid information overload. There is a point reached where too much information provides negative versus positive value. However, the technology is here. What and how much information should be accessed and how to interpret it will be determined by the business representative. It is up to the information technologist to provide fast, direct access to required information. The data warehouse is an information resource for modern business only if the information is accessible in a user-friendly and timely manner.

Summary

The key to corporate survival is obtaining knowledge before your competitors do. Therefore, data warehousing is the mission-critical project your corporation needs to embark on during the next few years.[22] Implementing a data warehouse successfully will be the key to providing timely data to business users. This book provides a jump start in interpreting data warehousing and other related information technologies.

The goal of this book is to interpret data warehouse technology for business managers. This book is written using nontechnical terms to provide accessible information for the business manager to determine whether or not the corporation needs a data warehouse. If the corporation currently has a data warehouse, the business manager can identify how to use or improve on the existing facility.

This chapter had three objectives, which all have the same goal: to provide sufficient information about data warehousing (the strategic tool for corprorate survival), showing how a business manager can greatly facilitate the development effort. Chapter 2, "How a Data Warehouse Is Built," provides an overview of the process of building a data warehouse to prepare the business manager for the development effort.

2

How a Data Warehouse Is Built

E xecutives will not argue that timely, quality data is crucial to a corporation's ability to be competitive in today's global market. However, executives want the bottom line. Chapter 1, "Data Warehousing," provided insight into the benefit side of the return on investment (ROI) equation. The other variable of ROI is cost.[1] To understand the underlying costs, the business manager is introduced to the process of building a data warehouse. To keep it simple, this process is explained in correlation to designing, building, and implementing any other type of product.

Building a data warehouse is a labor-intensive process. It takes experienced individuals to build and implement a data warehouse to satisfy evolving business needs. Generically, however, building a data warehouse is conceptually similar to building any other product. This chapter compares the process of building and implementing a data warehouse to that of the manufacturing process. Using the basic concepts of the manufacturing process, more specific detail will be provided to explain how to implement a data warehouse.

The detail is not at such an advanced level that it would allow a reader to build and implement a data warehouse on his or her own. The work of individuals trained in specific technologies is required. However, this chapter provides an overall understanding of how a data warehouse is built to facilitate the process and to determine whether or not the benefit outweighs the cost and work effort. By providing the business manager with a better understanding of the effort involved in such a project, he or she will have a better idea of the level of commitment required.

To explain how a data warehouse is built, this chapter describes the process in steps. Each step will have a purpose, input, output, and a brief description of the tasks that involve the business representative.[2]

The Manufacturing Process

The manufacturing of any product follows some type of process flow that produces the final product. The repeatable flow can be broken down into the following phases:

⇨ **Step 1:** The birth of an idea

  ⇨ **Step 2:** Analyze its feasibility

    ⇨ **Step 3:** Design the product

      ⇨ **Step 4:** Develop the product

        ⇨ **Step 5:** Assemble and test the product

          ⇨ **Step 6:** Implement the product

            ⇨ **Step 7:** Maintain and enhance the product

              ⇨ **Step 8:** Discontinue the product

The design, development, and testing of the product (steps 3 through 5) may have many iterations. Each iteration, called *prototyping*, refines the requirements or design of the final product. The product continues its life until it is discontinued. Until that time, fixing defects after the product's implementation is called *maintenance*. Adding new features to future models is called *enhancement*. Wrapped around the manufacturing process are the planning and management of the final product's ultimate delivery. The whole approach is a repeatable process filled with quality checkpoints to ensure that the best possible product is delivered to the customer.

Building a Data Warehouse

Building a data warehouse should not be viewed differently than the manufacturing process. It follows the same repeatable process flow:

⇨ **Step 1:** The birth of a need and use for a data warehouse

  ⇨ **Step 2:** Analyzing the feasibility and ROI of building a data warehouse

⇨ **Step 3:** Designing the data warehouse

⇨ **Step 4:** Developing the data warehouse

⇨ **Step 5:** Assembling and testing the data warehouse

⇨ **Step 6:** Implementing the data warehouse

⇨ **Step 7:** Maintaining and enhancing the data warehouse.

⇨ **Step 8:** Obsolescence of the data warehouse

As with the building of any product, the design, development, and testing of a data warehouse will have many iterations. The product continues its life until it becomes obsolete. Until that time, fixing defects after implementation is called *maintenance*. Adding new features to future releases is called making *enhancements*. For a data warehouse, these enhancements may be in the form of *incremental implementations*, which reduce the financial and time constraints associated building and implementing a data warehouse while benefitting the corporation at planned stages.[3] Obsolescence of a data warehouse occurs because there is a lack of need for its data contents or from outdated technology. In either case, it has been determined that the continual cost of maintaining and enhancing the current data warehouse outweighs its benefits and usefulness.

As with the manufacturing process, there is a plan for building and developing a data warehouse that manages the ultimate delivery of each incremental implementation. The whole approach is a repeatable process filled with quality checkpoints to ensure that the requirements (information, cost, and delivery) are being met. The process is repeatable for each iteration of the incremental implementation.

In general terms, this is how a data warehouse is built. It conceptually follows a similar process to building any product. Before building a data warehouse, it is important to understand in specific detail how one is actually built. This knowledge will enable the reader to determine if the effort is worth the benefit or to have sufficient understanding to facilitate its development. Each step in building a data warehouse will be discussed in more detail along with a brief description of the inputs and outputs at each step, the players involved, and the role they play.

Step 1: The Birth of an Idea

A change in corporate direction has created a new strategy that focuses on customer profiling and market segmentation. However, this strategy requires analyzing complex information manually. The information comes from multiple sources both internal and external to the corporation. The accuracy of the information is questionable as the same type of information has different values from the different sources. The amount of time and energy that a corporation spends achieving its current business objectives precludes any opportunity to identify new trends or opportunities.

An idea is born that a data warehouse is the answer to this problem. The information is brought inhouse and the data is cleaned to obtain accuracy and reduce decision-making time. As with any product development process, a need has been identified. In this case, a data warehouse becomes the viable solution.

From talking with colleagues or reading business publications, you might decide that a data warehouse is the technological solution to your information needs. By now it is apparent that a data warehouse is not something one can buy off the shelf at a local computer store. It is a system that requires a significant amount of resources, finances, and technology to build and implement.

Again, the need or idea for a data warehouse will develop from divisional or corporate strategy and from the pain and frustration of attempting to accomplish your own job. Cleansing data for consistency is an added benefit but never the sole reason for implementing a data warehouse. Therefore, do the time and cost involved outweigh the need for one?

Data Warehousing Advice for Managers provides enough information to determine whether or not your corporation should invest in building a data warehouse. You will be able to identify how the data warehouse can be used and by whom. At this point, you will have enough information to initiate a business case. You are ready to approach management for permission to spend time and resources to build a business case. You are now ready to determine the feasibility of building a data warehouse for your corporation.

Information technicians usually do not participate in this process. However, you may wish to take this opportunity to become familiar with someone in your information technology department who is familiar with data warehousing. Spend some time with this individual discussing your idea and identify any data warehouse projects that are currently being undertaken by your organization.

The input for this step of the process is to identify need *(analysis of complex customer and marketing data)*. Before asking management to further investigate the data warehouse solution, you must have a concept of the need that is tied to corporate or departmental strategy need *(cus-*

tomer profiling and market segmentation). Clarify your current situation and any weaknesses in it *(manual analysis process using conflicting data)*. Propose how the data warehouse will tactically provide answers to strategic questions *(reduce the time to identify new markets and customer purchasing patterns)*.

This step, the birth of an idea, entails clarifying the need. This includes defining the scope of what kind of data the data warehouse will contain. This means identifying the business subject areas (such as customer profiles or point-of-sale data) and the data required to support those areas.

Another task to be accomplished during this step is to become familiar with what a data warehouse is and what it can do for the corporation. You will become a spokesperson on the topic. You will be the primary source of information for noninformation technology personnel. By reading this book, you will have enough information to assist you in describing a data warehouse to your staff, peers, and management.

The output from this step is the request[4] you submit to your manager to investigate the feasibility of implementing a data warehouse to satisfy current needs. The request should contain a description of what a data warehouse is and how you believe it will help the current situation.

Figure 2-1 summarizes the purpose, inputs, outputs, and the role of business and information technology for this step. Step 1 is primarily executed by the business manager who discovered the need for a data warehouse. Talk with peers who have been involved in a data warehouse implementation.

Figure 2-1. Summary of step 1: birth of an idea.

Purpose:	To define the need for a data warehouse.
Input:	Current weaknesses with the current data analysis process.
Output:	Document in a request to management for time to investigate the feasibility of a data warehouse solution. This includes a description of what a data warehouse is and the weaknesses of the current process.
Business:	Produce the request to proceed to the next step.
Information Technology:	Basic information on data warehousing and identifying other business areas that are currently using this type of facility.

Step 2: Analyzing the Feasibility

Once you have received approval to investigate the feasibility (and more importantly the ROI) of implementing a data warehouse, you will be able to develop a successful business case with the assistance of information technology.[5] The business case will provide enough information for the executive management committee to determine if the data warehouse project should be initiated. With the information contained in the business case, they will agree to allocate resources and create a budget so that you can continue to the next step. The objective of this step is only to obtain funding and resources to complete Step 3.

According to Dr. Howard Rubin, a leading information technology expert and adviser to President Bill Clinton, for every dollar spent on information technology, thirty cents constitutes a non-value–producing expense. Over the next year (specifically due to the Year 2000 crisis), Rubin predicts the non-value–producing total to rise to fifty-five cents.[6]

With this financial information in mind, it is imperative to fully analyze the feasibility of building a data warehouse in your organization before you agree to implementing one. The tangible and intangible benefits must be clearly defined as well as the estimated costs. With this information, executive management will be able to determine the ROI to grant the continuance of the project through to the next step.

Developing the business case will require the assistance of information technologists, who will assist you in defining the scope of and the activities involved in implementing a data warehouse, and in estimating associated costs. It is important to define obtainable business performance measures that are expected to improve as a result of having implemented a data warehouse. Providing executive management with information about the success of data warehouses will encourage its members to continue their support throughout the incremental implementation process.

Developing a formal business case requires the input of information concerning the following:

- Business goals and objectives

- Current data needs (internal and external to the corporation) and usage within each business area that the data warehouse will support

- Examples of usage for each piece of data (including its shortcomings or inconsistencies)

- Volume (such as the number of products or customers) of each piece of data

- Level of detail (every transaction or monthly summaries) of each piece of data

- Frequency with which the user requires (first week of the month) the data

- Frequency in which the data must be updated (daily)

- List of possible users, their geographical locations, and level of expertise

- Timeliness or how up-to-date the information must be to be valuable to the decision-making process

Do not rely on information technologists to determine important business data, because they understand technology, not business. In fact, they will probably not become direct users of the data warehouse. Therefore, all they can tell you is whether or not the information exists in current production systems. Only business knowledge experts will understand the data and how to interpret it.

The opposite is true with data-intensive professionals because the vast majority of these individuals will be indirect information consumers rather than direct data analysts. An example of an indirect user is an executive requesting bottom-line results. Therefore, when determining what data to capture and how to clean it, remember that only a small percentage of business data analysts will actually use the data warehouse directly.

Figure 2-2 summarizes the purpose, inputs, outputs, and the role of business and information technology for this step. The business manager is still the driving force. However, only information technologists can correctly determine the costs involved in implementing a data warehouse.

Figure 2-2. Summary of step 2: analyzing the feasibility.

Purpose:	To define the feasibility of implementing a data warehouse at your organization.
Input:	Approval for the feasibility and the information contained on the formal request.
Output:	Formal business case and presentation.
Business:	Define the scope and tangible benefits; produce the formal business case and presentation.
Information Technology:	Could be either a data analyst, business information analyst, requirements engineer, and/or project leader who supplies the cost and first-cut project schedule.

Step 3: Designing the Data Warehouse

The data warehouse design will also go through the following five steps in the iterative process:

1. Identify business areas.

2. Define the data content of each business area.

3. Understand which data are important to decision making.

4. Identify the ultimate source of the data.

5. Develop a model of the data warehouse.

Accomplishing these steps leads to a better understanding of the scope of the project and its projected cost. The time spent is crucial to the success of the data warehouse. The design step of the data warehouse process identifies facts about the data that will need to be stored in the data warehouse, including associated dimensions[7] that will support drill-down and drill-across inquiry of data. Figure 2-3 illustrates data dimen-

Figure 2-3. The data warehouse cube.

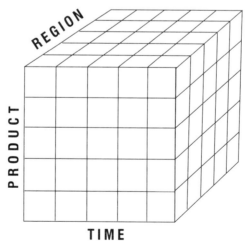

sions. Once the fact and dimension tables have been defined, the source of the data will be identified.

The business knowledge experts of each business subject area included in the data warehouse scope must provide:

- *The basic nature of the data.* What type of data will be utilized? Archival data, existing systems data, and future changes are all possibilities.

- *Attribute mapping.* The process of defining the data warehouse's data item characteristics (attributes). This process includes mapping to current versions of the data from source transactional systems. The current versions of the data items will serve as the source of the data values when populating[8] the data warehouse. The source represents transactional system storage and the target represents the data warehouse. This includes:

  — Use of a default value when a value is not present in the source system (dummy account or invoice number)

  — Attribute-to-attribute mapping (one-for-one match between source and target)

  — Multiple-attributes to one-attribute mapping (calculation of the source data to arrive at the result to be stored in the target)

  — Attribute conversion attribute (numeric to character, logical conversion, algorithmic conversion, etc.)

- *Summarization.* Will single data items be mapped directly to the data warehouse or will some degree of summarization be performed (daily values stored as monthly summaries)?

- *Frequency of transformation.* How often will the transformation of data occur?

- *Occurrence mapping.* Will all source records or only selected source records result in the creation of a data warehouse record (each transaction or one-in-five)?

- *Volume.* How much data will be maintained in the data warehouse? What is the level of granularity? How often will source records be scanned?

- *Sequence.* When only selected records or summarized records are passed to the data warehouse, what is the sequence?

The business knowledge expert provides a detailed definition of the characteristics of the data that will be stored in the data warehouse. He or she also decides which source represents the valid data. This decision is crucial when there are multiple files and data structures with customer information. The business community will decide which source and data are correct and complete.

During this phase the underlying architecture of the data warehouse is determined. Information technology analysts will ask questions about data type, format, and use. Business terms need to be clarified in addition to any business policies and rules that the data organization represents. The architectural drawings developed during this phase contain notation that both the business and information technologist understand. The final "business" model should represent the business without any technological constraints.

The information discussing the data, its characteristics, and any associated business constraints is so important that it is the biggest chunk of the data warehouse's business requirements.[9] Therefore, clearly and concisely defining the business model is crucial to successfully implementing a data warehouse.

To ensure that the business requirements are understood, the business manager must carefully review the output developed by information technologists. This can be done by reviewing the business model, which contains the following information:

- A diagram using standard notation to imply the things that are important to the business area. Only those things that are within the scope are included. The notation documents the relationship between these things and the business policies and rules that the data warehouse must enforce. The diagram is a form of architectural drawing for building a house.

- A business description of each thing that is important to the business area. An example of a "thing" would be a product or customer.

- What attributes describe each thing. An example of the attribute for product would be product number, product type, and product description. An example of customer would be customer number and customer name.

- Each attribute would have a business description.

The best source for each data item is determined as well as the targeted stored format.

The criteria for determining the source of the data should be the following:

- What data is the most accurate?

- What data is the most complete?

- What data is the most timely?

- What data most closely conforms to the structure of the data warehouse model?

- What data is nearest to the originating source?

Figure 2-4 summarizes the purpose, inputs, outputs, and the role of business and information technology for this step. In summary, the data warehouse design will use the following iterative process:

1. Finalizing the business subject areas

2. Defining the data content of each business area

3. Understanding which data are important to decision making

4. Identifying the ultimate sources of the data

5. Developing a business model of the data warehouse

Figure 2-4. Summary of step 3: designing the data warehouse.

Purpose:	To clearly define the infrastructure of the data warehouse.
Input:	Scope of the data warehouse.
Output:	Data warehouse infrastructure.
Business:	Specifically, the business knowledge experts will identify the data to be stored, determine the characteristics of the data, and select the source.
Information Technology:	Using data-modeling techniques will develop the infrastructure for the data warehouse.

Step 4: Developing a Data Warehouse

According to a survey of information technologists who are involved in data warehousing, 40 percent of the biggest challenges are with technology.[10] The need to interface new with old technologies includes the integration, extraction, and access into existing legacy (old) systems.

The physical environment can make or break a data warehouse. Besides being one of the biggest cost components of implementation, the architecture to support the data must provide sufficient access speeds to the information. Business users will become disillusioned and revert to old ways of retrieving data if response time is slow.

The hardware strategy must also anticipate growth in usage and data needs. If not, the entire data warehouse project may be jeopardized. If the data warehouse is deployed in a manner that is incapable of growing with future needs, the architecture and infrastructure[11] may need to be replaced. If this occurs, you will lose executive support and be unable to deliver a positive ROI.

This step involves imposing the technology onto the design developed during the previous phase. A great deal of leg work is accomplished by the information technologist who determines the most cost-effective technological platform that fits the corporation's needs. The business requirements are refined even further and developed into implementable design features.

Second, the modified business model[12] represents what information will be stored and how. The business model is modified into a physical model to make optimal use of the technological architecture. Indexes, or pointers to the data, are identified based on the most common user access requirements to facilitate response time to the most commonly used inquiries.

Third, the business users and their location must be determined to develop a logistics model of the network required. What will be required by the business manager and at what time will it need to be clarified? This information is used to design the partitioning and distributing plan, and schedule the data targeted for the data warehouse.

The physical architecture of the data warehouse can represent a three-tier or two-tier framework,[13] which refers to where the data resides and is accessed and how many stops there are along the way. This information is important to the business manager who will be asked, in more detail, what type of information will be required by each business user's location and how and when it will be accessed. These logistics impact on the cost of the physical architecture as well as the response time requirements.

The point-to-point connection could pass through several hubs or connection points. Each connection point could be a different hardware platform. The data does not necessarily need to all be contained at one location but can either be distributed (including replication) or partitioned to reside at several connection points. The two- or three-tier architecture is correlated to the connection points.

Two-tier architecture has the data for the data warehouse in one place. Figure 2-5 illustrates the two-tier view. Business users submit their inquiries and they are processed from one central point. There are only two points between the business user's location and the central source for the data warehouse's information.

Figure 2-5. Two-tier data warehouse architecture.

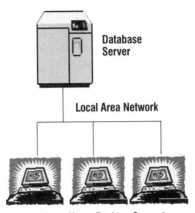

The benefit is that the information is kept and managed in one place. The side effect can be delayed response time due to concurrent access by many business users who need the same data simultaneously.

Different business users have different data needs. One group may require the details of specific sale transactions while another group may require monthly summaries. These different data needs could present another response time delay due to unnecessary processing for the business users who require summarized information. The extra process of continually summarizing the information is unnecessary but required due to the business users who require detail for their analyses.

Three-tier architecture, as depicted in Figure 2-6, allows for tailoring the process to a business user's specific needs. The data is managed from a central source. Managing the data includes retrieving it from the source and cleansing it. Then the central controller either distributes the data to different connection points or partitions (slices) it to the different connection points, or a combination of both methods.

Distributing the data sends an exact replica or aggregated format of a subset of the central repository to the file server that supports specific

Figure 2-6. Three-tier data warehouse architecture.

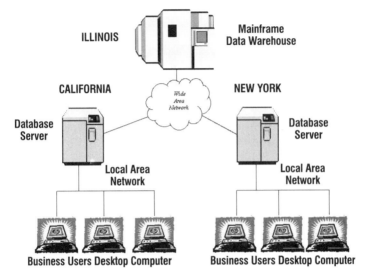

business-user locations. The information does not replace what is in the central source. For example, the central data warehouse contains all sales transactions for the year. What is stored on your specific local file server could be a summation of monthly sale figures for your geographic area. It depends on the needs of your business unit as compared to the needs of the corporation.

Replication of data[14] is required by businesses that need data availability or performance improvements at remote sites. The benefit is quicker response time and less concurrency access restriction. Its limitation is that inquiries cannot be made across different business locations but need to go between the specific locations and the central source. The weakness is the duplication of data between the central source and all the different business-user locations and the processing required to maintain two locations of data. The data could become inconsistent. Again, the problem of which data is correct could reemerge. This problem impacts on the cost of data warehouse storage and data maintenance.

Partitioning is the term used to describe the process of breaking up the data warehouse into logical blocks.[15] Partitioning sends pieces or slices of the data to reside on the file servers supporting specific business-user locations. Each file server does not have to be the same technological platform to provide the ability to leverage existing hardware at end-user locations. No data resides in a central source. Every file server contains the information it requires. Access is permitted for inquiries that span business-user locations. Partitioning reduces redundancy but becomes a networking nightmare. Response time can be impacted depending upon the number of locations containing needed data that must be accessed. The decision of whether to use two- or three-tier architecture should be made by the information technology organization. This decision, however, is based upon the end user's requirements and budget. The business manager who is accountable for the success of the data warehouse implementation should have a conceptual understanding of these architectures. This understanding will facilitate communication between the information technologists, yourself, and the executive manager who is paying the bill.

Usually, it is during this step that the data warehouse's physical architecture is precisely defined. The physical architecture includes all hardware, network configurations, security requirements, end-user tools, and all tangible pieces of the data warehouse. Figure 2-7 summarizes the purpose, inputs, outputs, and the role of business and information technology for this step. Information technology takes a primary role during this step. However, it is important for the business manager to stay involved to ensure that the requirements identified are satisfied by the architecture.

Figure 2-7. Summary of step 4: developing the data warehouse.

Purpose:	To develop the physical architecture for the data warehouse, network, and associated tools.
Input:	Data warehouse infrastructure.
Output:	Physical design (architecture), hardware, and software order, if necessary.
Business:	To resolve any data cleansing and data usage issues. Begin developing end-user training. Assist in the selection of end-user tools. Knowledge experts will assist in any partitioning schemes for specific business areas.
Information Technology:	Design the data warehouse's physical architecture.

Step 5: Assembling and Testing the Data Warehouse

Assembly is not easy. Data from its original source may not be in proper format or may require modifications. In other words, data must be cleansed before it can be placed in the data warehouse. The specifications for the cleansing process were developed during the previous step. However, issues always arise when actual coding begins.

The business users of this targeted data warehouse must be the individuals who test it. They are the business knowledge experts who understand the data and its usage. Only they will be able to determine if the results of the inquiries are what was expected. Testing involves reviewing the data for cleansing and aggregation accuracy. If partitioning was used, the business knowledge experts must verify that the correct data went to the correct location in the proper format. The users of the data must validate that the statistical and reporting tools or predefined inquiries are correctly manipulating the data. Response times need to be measured to identify any network or design performance problems.

This is also a good point at which to determine the business user's educational requirements. Even the best designed and implemented data warehouse will fail if proper training does not take place. Plan training for different levels of users. Do not attempt to satisfy all your training needs with one class.[16]

Figure 2-8 summarizes the purpose, inputs, outputs, and the role of business and information technology for this step.

Figure 2-8. Summary of step 5: assembling and testing the data warehouse.

Purpose:	To assemble and test the data warehouse's contents and architecture.
Input:	Specifications about the technical architecture.
Output:	Working data warehouse.
Business:	Business knowledge experts must test the results of common inquiries. Train the future users of the data warehouse.
Information Technology:	Develop and test the data warehouse.

Step 6: Implementing a Data Warehouse

Implementing a data warehouse is no small task. All the hardware must be in place. All the business users must be trained, with access to their data. All the software for cleansing, distributing, and partitioning the data must be working accurately. "Rolling out" or "turning on" the data warehouse for general usage for the first time is the most stressful part of the entire implementation effort. Even when following the best practices for implementing a data warehouse, this step is what executive management remembers most.

Final implementation of this incremental release must be left to the information technologist. During this time, the businessperson must gather statistics to prove that the data warehouse was successful and that continual incremental implementations provide value to the corporation. The businessperson must look out for:

- How businesspeople work and what data warehouse tools and data could help them to be more successful

- What business problems the next incremental release should be geared toward solving

- What additional training or special hand-on assistance will help specific business users

Figure 2-9 summarizes the purpose, inputs, outputs, and the role of business and information technology for this step.

Figure 2-9. Summary of step 6: implementing a data warehouse.

Purpose:	Implement the data warehouse.
Input:	Implementation plan.
Output:	A usable data warehouse.
Business:	Business user training. Statistics pertaining to the ROI validation.
Information Technology:	Implement the data warehouse.

Step 7: Maintaining and Enhancing the Data Warehouse

Maintenance items are both business needs and system needs. After the data warehouse is in production and being used by its targeted business community, statistics should be gathered as to the types of inquiries and data being accessed, and the response time. The information gained by monitoring data warehouse usage will provide documentation that the information technologist can use to determine if any performance enhancements can be made.

Implementing a data warehouse all at once is one of the most common reasons for failure.[17] However, many businesses have implemented their first incremental release and are convinced of a data warehouse's value. More business users than originally anticipated will come knocking at your door. This may include more data than was previously envisioned. Therefore, each incremental release must be reviewed for the following:

- Not stressing the network already in place

- Increasing training, storage, or other tangible costs

- Adding business value and providing a positive ROI

Once a data warehouse is providing data access and tools that satisfy analytical queries, your original plan of action for future incremental enhancements must be reviewed. When patterns are seen, relationships are uncovered, causality is quantified, and inferences are drawn, the data must be reviewed as to the value it is providing the organization. Your previous plan may need adjusting to accommodate the knowledge results achieved due to the data warehouse. This includes:

- Adding additional dimensions to the data that already exists in the data warehouse

- Providing more detail with data previously kept at a summary level

- Expanding the type of data stored for a specific business subject area

- Adding data for different business subject areas that were identified for the next release

- Providing additional tools that will mine[18] the data for additional information

All these decisions must be made by the business community and sold and approved by the executive committee. The original plan is not cast in stone. However, any adjustments in the previous approach should be associated with additional business justification (ROI).

This step is the beginning of the product development cycle minus the proof of concept. It is important to gather statistics and determine if the original estimates for ROI were accurate. They must be presented to the executive management with any request for the next incremental release.

Maintenance and enhancement must be carefully managed. Success the first time does not mean success for each subsequent incremental release. The process must be reviewed to clarify the reasons for success and to identify any areas where improvements can be made and used during the next implementation. Business must remain prominent during *every* incremental implementation to ensure that the releases are the best ones for the corporation.

Figure 2-10 summarizes the purpose, inputs, outputs, and the role of business and information technology for this step.

Figure 2-10. Summary of step 7: maintaining and enhancing the data warehouse.

Purpose:	The continue support of the implemented data warehouse.
Input:	New requirements, defects, performance monitoring statistics.
Output:	Plan for the next incremental release.
Business:	Supply new requirements, information about any defects, examples of trends in how business users are actually using the data warehouse.
Information Technology:	Resolve defects, develop a plan for the next incremental release.

Step 8: Obsolescence

A data warehouse becomes obsolete when it no longer provides value to the business community or the maintenance costs exceed any ROI. Outdated technology should never be the reason for obsolescence. For a price, platforms can be changed. New tools can be purchased to provide better performance or usability.

Figure 2-11 summarizes the purpose, inputs, outputs, and the role of business and information technology for this step.

Figure 2-11. Summary of step 8: obsolescence.

Purpose:	To determine the continual value of the data warehouse.
Input:	Statistics on usage and maintenance costs; current ROI.
Output:	Analysis of the effectiveness of the current data warehouse and recommendations for next steps.
Business:	ROI variables.
Information Technology:	Costs and recommended next steps.

The Importance of the Business Manager's Role

The role of the business manager in building a data warehouse is to provide information technologists with an understanding of what is needed, how it should be interpreted, and in what format it is required. They provide valuable insight into the targeted users of the data warehouse. They understand the needs of the business. Therefore, the business manager's role is to facilitate the process of implementing a successful data warehouse and to remain involved to ensure the most effective use by the business community.

Summary

This chapter described, at a very high level, how a data warehouse is built. It is similar to any manufacturing process. Your own corporation may already have a data warehouse that you may wish to expand upon. The process described in this chapter covers that given scenario. The purpose of this chapter was to provide the reader with enough detail:

- To understand the underlying labor costs

- To determine the importance of his or her role throughout the process

- To provide a comfort level for the business manager facilitating the effort

- To illustrate that the labor-intensive process does not outweigh the benefits of a data warehouse to the corporation

Data warehouses have been installed at many corporations that vary in size, complexity, and industry. Some have been successful and some have not. To avoid failures and to ensure success, Chapter 3, "Keys to a Successful Implementation," provides some simple techniques the business manager can use throughout the data warehouse process.

3

Keys to a Successful Implementation[1]

C hapter 2, "How a Data Warehouse Is Built," describes the eight-step process of building and maintaining a data warehouse. This chapter reviews topics the business manager should be aware of during the process to ensure its success. Data warehouse projects have a high risk of failure. Most causes could have been easily avoided by following some simple techniques, which fall into four basic categories:

Category A: *Business Knowledge* refers to anything related to conveying and confirming that the rules of the business are communicated, designed, verified, and implemented into the data warehouse.

Category B: *Management* has to do with business maintaining control of the data warehousing effort. Remember, information technology is there for the business and not the other way around.

Category C: *Process* relates to items that have to do with the eight-step process for building a data warehouse.

Category D: *Infrastructure* pertains to items that affect the underlying structure of the data warehouse.

Knowledge is control. Knowing what works and what fails will help the business manager control the data warehouse effort and ensure its success. This chapter will teach the business manager which techniques must be followed by the data warehousing team (business and technology) to achieve success. The business manager will learn how to identify the flags of possible failures before they happen.

The business manager already has a generous reservoir of knowledge at his or her fingertips that will facilitate the data warehouse's success. This knowledge is a combination of business practices, marketing strategies, basic management techniques, and common sense. This chapter will illustrate how to take that knowledge and reshape it for the needs of the data warehouse.

Business Knowledge

A data warehouse contains data about the business. Its organization enforces the rules, policies, and procedures of the business. Therefore, it is crucial that business personnel define their data warehousing requirements in a format that is understandable to the information technologist to avoid any misinterpretations. It is imperative that the project team understands the essential business process to be able to define the requirements. Therefore, it is important that business representatives who have comprehensive knowledge of the business be part of the data warehouse development team. To expand upon these points, the following are discussed:

- What are good requirements

- Understanding essential business processes

- User documentation

What Are Good Requirements?

Approximately 50 percent of failed information technology projects floundered because of requirements. Data warehouse projects are no exception. For this reason, it is important for the business manager to understand what a good requirement is. It will help the business manager to write and verify requirements that will impact the data warehouse project and to manage its scope.

Requirements are probably the most misunderstood and misinterpreted deliverable for a data warehouse project. Often, business managers believe that the requirements have already been presented. On the other side, information technologists believe that the requirements are too vague because they are unable to code directly from them. In reality, good requirements are somewhere in the middle of both points of view.

The business requirements start out in general terms. However, they must still be unambiguous and concise. Information technology will not be able to code from them (yet). Throughout the data warehouse development process, more detail is uncovered and additional requirements are derived that are crucial to support the original requirements. Requirements increase in number, level of detail, and amount of documentation before the data warehouse is actually implemented. Requirements evolve and must be traced and managed throughout the life of the data warehouse. This structure provides audit trails and eliminates future misunderstandings.

Careful management and review of the requirements must be monitored by the business manager to ensure that extraneous requirements are not incorporated into the project's scope.[2] Expanded scope may cause the project to fail by not satisfying the original need or by lowering the ROI.

Good requirements are essential for the success of the data warehouse. They facilitate the design, testing, implementation, and maintenance effort. Good requirements are imperative for achieving a ROI that the executives expect. For this reason, it is important for the business manager, as well as the information technologist, to know what a good requirement should contain. Figure 3-1[3] briefly describes the contents.

Requirements evolve through several steps of the development process. The gathering of requirements is an evolutionary subprocess within the development process. The subprocess[4] is:

- Elicitation

- Analysis

- Specification

- Validation

- Approval

During elicitation, requirements begin as high-level statements. Each statement is labeled for traceability. During analysis, each requirement statement is analyzed to determine the detail that will satisfy the requirement characteristic as described in Figure 3-1. Each requirement is then formally documented during specification, in some form and structure as depicted in Figure 3-2.[5] Requirement organization is important since it

Figure 3-1. Requirement characteristic checklist.

Characteristic	Brief Description	Data Warehouse Implication
Correctness	Each requirement should be correct in its statement of purpose.	Each requirement must state what the data warehouse will contain, groups it will support, actions that will be performed, and from what locations.
Unambiguous	Only one interpretation can be inferred from the requirement statement; no "to be determined" is allowed.	The information technologist will know exactly what data is needed when and where and what probable functions will be performed on that data including restricted access.
Complete	All significant information about the requirements must be included. For example, all data, process, performance, responses, and desired format must be included.	All data that is required for a view or calculation will be known. Any formulas to be performed on the data have been described.
Consistent	All requirements look the same and do not conflict with each other.	Every person supplying requirements uses the same format for describing each requirement.
Ranked for importance	Priority indicator, such as essential, conditional, and optional.	All requirements have agreement with the priority and implementation phase.
Ranked for stability	Are changes to this requirement expected.	Any requirement that may change due to organizational issues, new products and services, must be identified to forewarn the designers.
Verifiable	How will you test that this requirement has been satisfied?	State that calculated results must be within a certain percentage of accuracy to the detail. Include here any performance (response time or availability) restrictions or rounding impact limits.
Modifiable	The format of the requirement can be easily modified when changes occur.	Do not present a requirement using a tool that only one person has access to! Make sure that the requirement is depicted using a tool and format that all understand. Use automated tools instead of handwritten notes.
Traceable	Each requirement contains an identifier that can be traced through the development process. All changes to the requirement can also be traced to the original requirement.	Define a standard label for all requirements.

Reprinted from IEEE Std. 830–1993 "IEEE Recommended Practice for Software Requirements Specifications," Copyright © 1994, by the Institute of Electrical and Electronics Engineers, Inc. (IEEE).

Figure 3-2. Sample outline for a requirement specification.

I. Introduction

Purpose of this document

Scope of the data warehouse project

Business and data warehouse definitions, acronyms, and abbreviations

References to related business documentation and policies

Overview of the data warehouse system concept

Overall Description

Business perspective

Data warehouse functions

User characteristics

    Tools

    Access requirements

    Constraints*

    Assumptions and dependencies

Specific requirement covering: data, function, location, and any organizational impact.

*Constraints within a data warehouse requirements document should not pertain to project management activities such as schedule and budget. An example of a data warehouse constraint would be the availability of data from an outside provider to satisfy a report request.

Reprinted from IEEE Std. 830–1993 "IEEE Recommended Practice for Software Requirements Specifications," Copyright © 1994, by the Institute of Electrical and Electronics Engineers, Inc. (IEEE).

facilitates understanding by all data warehouse project team members. It may also be used, in part, for user documentation.

Validation is when all project participants review each requirement for completeness and correctness. Approval is given by the official signatures of all project team members that the requirements are complete, correct, and understood. However, this does not mean that the requirements are final and can not change. After approval, the requirements are "baseline" and any alterations (including additions) must be traced. They are then analyzed for their possible impact on other project deliverables, including the project schedule and the ROI analysis.

In step one of the eight-step process (the idea to build a data warehouse), executives are able to determine if a business case should be initiated. No matter how high-level it is, each requirement should be able to pass the checklist depicted in Figure 3-1 at this stage. By satisfying the checklist, the business is assured that everyone agrees to the initial requirements and scope of the data warehouse effort. Having concise business requirements that satisfy the checklist provides accountability checkpoints that can be used when validating the data warehouse's success. These are the initial business requirements for a data warehouse. During the analysis step of the data warehouse process, requirements are drilled down into more detail. These are still business requirements but they should be developed jointly with information technologists who are trained in requirement-gathering techniques (requirements engineering) for a data warehouse.

Good requirements are a major step in ensuring that the data warehouse is a success. Take time to develop them properly and use the checklist as a guide. Work with an experienced requirements engineer to facilitate the process.

Understanding Essential Business Processes

Good requirements can not be developed without sufficiently understanding the business process. Therefore, the business representative involved in the requirements process must be a knowledgable expert on the topic under discussion.

Over the years, information systems have become increasingly complex in both technological and business attributes. The first thing both systems and business must recognize is that neither even comes close to understanding the unique knowledge that the other brings to the table. Systems people are brought in to know either the system or the technology. Keeping up with the field of technology and software engineering is enough to keep technicians busy. Even if they have some business knowledge, technicians will not be as sensitive to the demands or priorities of business and its direction. It is impossible for technicians to understand business as well as the knowledge experts do. Businesspeople work within the business on a daily basis. It is easy for technicians to think they know the business, but all they really understand is what is currently implemented in existing systems. Therefore, information technicians can facilitate the requirements' process but business must have control of its contents.

Different techniques have been used by information technologists to compensate for a lack of knowledge about the business. These techniques help facilitate the elicitation of requirements. Two of the most common approaches are:[6]

1. Joint application development (JAD)

2. One-on-one

Joint application development (JAD)[7] sessions are lead by a facilitator, and are designed to bring together key people from business to focus their attention on requirements for a specific project. The higher the level of businesspeople attending the JAD, the more each JAD session will contribute to the project's success. It is important that the attendees understand the essential business processes, the data that is required, and the business interpretations of the data. When conflicts arise about interpretation, it is the objective of the JAD session to resolve them immediately.

Sometimes the size of the system prohibits scheduling the "right" people for a JAD. This is where one-on-one meetings come into play. Meetings need to be scheduled to interview the right businesspeople, which includes the executive sponsor,[8] knowledge experts, management involved in setting the new direction, and anyone who may use the data warehouse. After performing the interviews, the technician will weave together the additional and derived requirements for the system.[9] The outcome will be the specifications that must be reviewed and approved by the business members of the project team.

The facilitator who is eliciting the requirements will ask a series of questions no matter which technique is used. The questions fall into the following areas:

- *Business events.* Identify all the reasons for accessing the data warehouse. Correlate these reasons with work flows or business processes that may restrict the design. Include in the reasons any time factors for the requests (for example, end of each quarter or ad hoc). Document what problems are you attempting to solve. Note any series of inquiries involved with your research to identify any patterns that may streamline the design.

- *Data.* Identify all business subjects (for example, products) to be included in the scope. Include the details (what you need to know about it and at what level) of each business subject and what patterns or dimensions the data should represent.

- *Geographic locations.* Who needs access to the data warehouse and from where and when?

- *The user level.* To identify required tools and training. Identify the level of the user who will be using the data warehouse.

Each requirement should be documented separately following the format described previously. If available, additional documentation should be provided to the technician who will help explain any of the above areas (business events, data, geographic locations, and user levels). Examples are the business plan, department strategy, business term dictionary, research papers, and organization charts.

A great deal of detail will be needed from the knowledge experts. Therefore, it is important that the right businesspeople are involved. Although they may not be involved in identifying the initial requirements, they must be involved in providing the supporting detail. If a businessperson is selected due to his or her availability and does not have the proper knowledge, the data will be misinterpreted and requirements unsatisfied. This will cause the data warehouse to fail.

User Documentation

The best designed data warehouse will fail if the users find it too difficult to use. Therefore, time must be spent in developing user documentation. Once your system has been implemented, the most time-consuming activity is fielding questions from the user community. Your project is not complete until there is high quality user documentation available. You will be able to judge the quality over time by the types of questions asked by the data warehouse users.

When creating user documentation, you must write with the user's point of view in mind and avoid using overly technical terms. Avoid complex sentences. Include lists of steps for people to follow (for example, pictures, contact names, and telephone numbers). Reference additional information and maintain the documentation with the most up-to-date information.

The user documentation should be easily maintained. As the user becomes acquainted with the data warehouse, different questions will be raised. As new tools are added, different information will be required. Therefore, user documentation should be in a format that is easily maintained and distributed and should never be distributed only once and forgotten.

Management

The success of a data warehouse project can often be attributed to following practical management techniques. Due to the high risk associated with a data warehouse project, business must ensure that the following management techniques are in place:

- Executive support

- Clearly defined plan

- Leaving it up to information technologists

- Time over quality

- Out-of-control outsourcing

Executive Support

Studies have shown that the one factor that contributes to a project's failure is a lack of support from its executive sponsors. Resolutions need to be made outside the project manager's authority for those cross-organizational boundaries. The person who has this authority is the executive sponsor. Without this support, issues will go unresolved at a high level. Consequently, the scope of the project will be reduced, or worse, corrupted. The executive sponsor will:

- Ensure compliance to the business strategy.

- Ensure resource priority.

- Clarify business terms and rules.

- Ensure cooperation between business units and information technology.

Some of the data warehouse issues that usually require executive involvement are concurrent business terms and clarification of business rules (above the line of business level). The actual trick is to make certain that the executive sponsor understands the importance of making a decision versus not making a decision. If the project is stalled at a particular point, you will need to illustrate, in dollars and cents, the cost of not making a decision. Refer to Figure 3-3.

Information technology can be easily sidetracked. Requests for their services comes from all business units and it is impossible for the the information technologists to support them all. This is especially true with modifications required to support the Year 2000 and the European Monetary Unit. For this reason, the executive sponsor must continually check to ensure that the data warehouse project remains on information technology's current list of responsibilities.

Figure 3-3. ROI checkpoint.

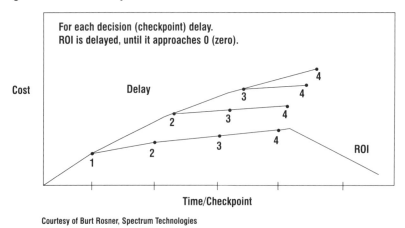

For each decision (checkpoint) delay.
ROI is delayed, until it approaches 0 (zero).

Cost

Delay

Time/Checkpoint

Courtesy of Burt Rosner, Spectrum Technologies

The executive sponsor must be kept informed of the project. Issues that require his or her attention must be clearly stated, optional answers provided, and a data set for which the resolution must be made.

Clearly Defined Plan

Every project that involves two or more people needs a documented plan to provide structure, scheduling, and organization. The more people or groups of people involved, the more clarity is required in the plan. The plan starts with a documented goal. The internals of the plan will address the objectives. The objectives will contain time frames (for example, hours, days, weeks, or months), resources (for example, people, hardware, or communications), and material (for example, paper, ink, tapes, or computer disks). All objectives will be linked either in sequential or parallel construction, or a combination of both depending on what needs to be accomplished and how it will be accomplished. The level of detail (clarity) will depend on the number of disciplines (for example, programmers, client/server experts, marketing, sales, or accounting) required. In short, the more disciplines involved with the project, the more your terminology will need to be clearly defined. Sensitivity to planning is paramount. The plan will be developed jointly with information technologists.

A project plan also includes a description of roles and responsibilities for all who participate in the data warehouse project. As your project proceeds, there will be a number of people performing a variety of tasks at any given time. Without knowing who is responsible for what, your project will automatically default to mass confusion. In order to avoid this scenario, you will need to document the type of work needed and who will be responsible for doing it. For large projects such as data warehousing, the cast of characters can be overwhelming. Talk with both business and systems people about what work needs to be accomplished and who will do it. Review the list in Figure 3-4 to make certain that you did not forget anyone.

Figure 3-4. Data warehouse roles.

• Business Analyst	• Project Manager
• Client Support	• Project Sponsor
• Conceptual Data Analyst	• Repository Administrator
• Conceptual Process Analyst	• Software Support
• Developer	• Subject Matter Expert
• Internal Auditor	• System Architect
• Methodologist (incl. Standards)	• Technical Support
• Physical Data Analyst	• Training
• Physical Process Analyst	

Time Over Quality

When push comes to shove, quality[10] always suffers. Unfortunately, getting something done is more important than the workmanship, or quality, required to be successful. If you find yourself among team members who are focusing on completing the project in the shortest amount of time possible, you know that you will not have a quality product. The system you are building will be a reflection of the way in which you conduct yourself and the type of products you are allowing to be associated with your name. A product with low quality means that your standards are not high. The business community will see this and think twice abut using your product or asking you to participate on another system. Worse yet, your next request for an information technology solution to a business problem will be ignored. Ensure quality by reviewing all documentation at each checkpoint.

On the opposite side of the coin is "analysis paralysis." This is a term used by the systems area to indicate that too much up-front thinking is going on and not enough real work is being performed. If analysis paralysis is tolerated, it will have a negative impact on your data warehouse project's ROI.

Obviously, there has to be a middle ground. The problem is deciding where it is. You can identify the middle ground by using three tools:

1. Requirements

2. Time

3. Percentage

Analysis begins with a review of the initial requirements. Analysis continues with the identification of conditions required to meet the expectations of those requirements. Sometimes the conditions are simple to address, sometimes not. The simple conditions are not responsible for stalling the project, or creating analysis paralysis. For example, a requirement states that a business area wants to use deferred payment. Each discipline has a different interpretation of "deferred payment." You are going to need to resolve a basic business rule of your company to clear up this requirement conflict. This is where time comes into play. You need to set a time limit as to when the issue will be resolved. This holds true for all requirements. After a specific time has elapsed, the percentage factor begins. How many issues were resolved? What is the percentage of issues resolved versus the total number of issues? If it is less than 80 percent, you have analysis paralysis.

Leaving It Up to Information Technologists

At some time during the data warehouse process, business managers will interface with technicians. Since your expertise is either advertising or sales, you might feel a little out of place dealing with the intricacies of building a data warehouse. It is very easy to look for someone in systems you can trust and let him or her take over the project. Whenever that thought enters your mind, you have just sealed the fate of the project. It is not that systems personnel will do something wrong, it is just that they really do not know what you want. You may explain it in great detail, but unless you participate, review, and verify what the system is supposed to do, it will fail. Remember, technicians know technology. Business managers know the business. The data warehouse is being implemented to support the business!

If you do go the route of letting the systems group do the leg work, you will need to review all their recommendations. Information technologists might purchase tools of their choice versus what the user requires. You will need to document, in detail, the features and functionality of what the business community tools should be. Then, when information technologists make a recommendation, you can easily compare the tool versus what you documented.

Out-of-Control Outsourcing

When a company gives work to a noncompany person or group that was formerly performed in the company, it is called outsourcing. A company will outsource work when it makes sense to do so. For example, it is not uncommon for a small company to have another company perform its payroll. Generally, the other company can perform the work better, cheaper, or more efficiently. However, out-of-control outsourcing occurs if a company does not know whether or not it is to the company's advantage to do it, or when there is poor communication during the development phase.

How does that affect your project? What if your systems development (for example, coding, testing, or reporting) work is performed by a software house and you are not a high priority for them? It is not that easy to switch, especially if the company has other production work that it is performing for you. If you find yourself in this scenario, you will need to factor in additional project time and hope it does not impact the original benefit of the project. It can not be stressed enough, business must review all interim documentation to ensure compliance to the requirements.

Managing Checkpoints

Throughout this management section, the importance of checkpoints has been stressed. Checkpoints are specific times during the data warehouse development at which everyone stops and reviews the work already completed. *Milestone* is another word used to mean the same thing. Checkpoints are inserted into your project plan when a major function or deliverable of the data warehouse has been completed. To be on the safe side, you will want to schedule reviews after each minor, but critical, function is completed. Be careful. If you include too many checkpoints, then all you will be doing is reviewing the project instead of getting anything accomplished. Insert checkpoints into your project plan when critical or dependent documentation is due for completion (for example, the business model).

Do not confuse this with status meetings. Checkpoints are a verification that a specific part of the data warehouse is correct in satisfying the requirements. A status meeting will discuss the progress the project is making.

Process

The process category refers to the steps and activities associated with designing, building, and implementing a successful data warehouse. In this category, four success items shall be discussed:

1. Poor software process

2. Information architecture

3. Conversion and integration

4. Easy-to-use tools

Poor Software Process

Poor software process is a term used to politely say that technicians are not following established rules and procedures for building programs, or using naming standards to describe the function of the programs, or that there are no policies or procedures to follow. In systems organizations where policies and procedures are not followed, you will generally find that 85 to 95 percent of the money you allocate each year for systems work actually goes into maintaining existing systems. The funds are not used to build new enhancements or create new and more efficient systems. For the systems people to improve their work practices, they will need support from you. You will need to ensure that policies and procedures are established and followed. You will need to ensure that there is a budget line with enough money to maintain the policies and procedures. You will need to support your systems area by allowing them additional time to perform the work. If you can do that, then you will see a sharp improvement. Ensure that the process, with standards, is defined *before* the step is executed. Insist that the process contains checkpoints and milestones for you to validate that the data warehouse will conform to the business requirements.

Information Architecture

Information architecture is the foundation of a data warehouse. Information architecture is the grouping of information (a.k.a. data) your company uses by the way the information is used (a.k.a. data relationships). After you have defined the scope of your project, you will need to develop an information architecture.

By identifying what information is available from various organizations in your company and relating that information, you can demonstate the type and structure of the information that will be provided from the data warehouse you are building. It does not matter that you are using the latest technology to access the information faster if the information itself is not wanted. For example, human resources is not only interested in knowing an employee's name. They also need to know when the employee started work, their salary grade, and home address. On the other hand, when a business decides to venture into a new line of work, they want to know what skills (expertise) the company already has in that field and at what level. By designing this association into the data warehouse's structure (an employee associated with a date of hire, mailing address, skill type and level) you have just created the beginnings of an information architecture that can be used by both human resources and the strategic planning group. The more information you can link (relate) the more robust your data warehouse will be.

Conversion and Integration

Most of the work you will be concerning yourself with when developing a data warehouse is the conversion and integration of data that are currently in different physical locations (for example, New York, Chicago, and Houston), databases (for example, DB2, Sybase, and Oracle), formats (for example, Alpha, Alpha/Numeric, and Numeric), and timing. This does not include the organizations that own or control the data, or the business units that use the data. The ability to bring all the data into one physical area, or linking all the various locations, databases, and formats together to maintain data integrity, is a goal of the data warehouse project. As a businessperson, you are required to understand the different descriptions of data that have the same name, and to identify data with different names that have the same description. You need to understand where the data is coming from, which data are accurate, what checks are being made to maintain the data, and how that data relates to other data. Once that is accomplished, you need to work with the systems people on how to collect, or link, the data in the most economical way and maintain its integrity at the same time. The impact of not following this procedure will produce the same environment you are currently working in, except you will be doing it with very expensive software tools.

The systems area will present this problem to you and, hopefully, recommend strategies and software tools to achieve your goal. The best way you can manage this is to initiate contacts with the business area using the data and give its members an opportunity to express how they want to view the data and what they will do once they can access it. You do not need to know the details of how that will be accomplished. You are responsible for making sure that what you deliver to the business areas can be used in the most economical way. Remember that there will be a trade-off as to what can be provided and its cost. If no resolution is achieved, then it is time to call in the executive sponsor.

Easy-to-Use Tools

Generally, people think of tools as items used for performing physical labor. A hammer is readily identified as a tool. When building a data warehouse, the word tool has the same meaning. Data warehouses are built and accessed using tools. Business is interested in data access tools. The tools selected must be easy to use. If they are not, the data warehouse will not be used and thus fail.

On the business side, you will be using word processors, spreadsheets, and analytical and user interface tools to access the data and recombine it to meet your needs. These tools are commonly referred to as data warehouse front-end software packages. Although there is no one "generic" software package to reference, there are specific features that you need. The following list is also discussed in Chapter 4, "What Do I Do With It Now?"

- Predefined reporting

- Simple ad hoc queries

- On-line analytical queries

- Multidimensional investigation

- Mathematical or statistical analysis

The predefined reporting feature allows you to purchase preformatted reports that can easily be used to access the data warehouse's information. However, since everyone has their own specific point of view, a more sophisticated customizable feature should also be included when purchasing a software package for report purposes.

The simple ad hoc queries feature allows you to access data based on one or two key words. Looking up customer information, creating mailing labels, viewing inventory are types of work that you can do with this feature.

The on-line analytical queries feature allows you to spot business trends using your desktop or laptop computer. Within a data warehouse environment these trends could literally be in a real-time mode. Some examples are inventory analysis, and local, national, and international sales trends.

The multidimensional investigation feature allows you to have more than two views on a chart. For example, you can view sales by region, person, or product within a specific time frame.

The mathematical or statistical analysis feature extrapolates historical data, given specific parameters, into possible future scenarios.

When building a data warehouse, businesspeople need to focus their attention on how the information will be presented, distributed, and interpreted. You need to discuss with the technicians what types of tools are available and how you can use those tools to obtain and read data. When talking with technicians, you need to keep the following in mind:

- How fast can the business community learn this tool?

- Does this tool work with other tools that the business community uses?

- How much does it cost and what is the business community getting for the price?

- How long will the business community be able to use the tool before the tools need to be "upgraded"?

- Who will help the business community when they have questions?

- What level of computer literacy (expertise) will the prospective users need to have before accessing the data warehouse?

Do not think that a tool is best for you because it is the latest one out on the market. It all comes back to you knowing which tools and what kind of environment you need. Identify the tool requirements before initiating the search. These requirements should be defined in the same format as other business requirements.

How to Test the Data Warehouse

Testing the data warehouse is composed of three parts:

1. Identifying the data warehouse environment that you are testing

2. Creating a test package

3. Documenting expected results

Identifying the data warehouse environment focuses your attention on the type of input and formats the system will be able to accept and the type of response time you feel is acceptable. Test packages for a data warehouse environment should be created to address both interactive (on-line queries and updates) and batch (queries and updates) scenarios. The on-line portion will require you to write a script that the testers will follow. The script consists of attempts to generate all data warehouse messages, including error messages, and what a person should do when a particular message appears. Batch tests consist of creating input records to verify that specific update and cross-checking functions work correctly. For example, your data warehouse requires an outside vendor to supply one of the pieces of information for your data warehouse. You will need to check the input format, accuracy, timeliness, and error handling portions of the system.

Documenting expected results for each test scenario will give you a figurative yardstick for measuring what the data warehouse is doing and what you can expect the system to do. The expected results will be compared to the actual results after the test. If there are differences, you will be required to resolve them. The procedures for resolving expected test results with actual test results should follow these three steps:

1. Check the specifications that the testers are using with the specifications the developers were using.

2. Verify which specification is correct.

3. Make corrections either to the test package or to the data warehouse's infrastructure or procedures.

Infrastructure

Infrastructure is the model that includes the technical architecture as well as the software to support the data warehouse. Pieces of the infrastructure model include areas that can be easily controlled by the business manager to ensure a successful implementation. These items are:

- Garbage in, garbage out

- Insufficient network capability

- All or nothing

- Unanticipated growth

Garbage in, Garbage Out

"Garbage in, garbage out" is more commonly known as GIGO, within systems. Every system, without exception, has three basic parts: input, process, and output. GIGO represent two of those parts, specifically input and output. If the data you are inputting is not accurate (the technical term is *garbage*), and you believe the process will somehow transform the data into something usable, you might have a surprise or two when you receive the output and can not make any sense of it (a.k.a. garbage). This particular problem compounds itself by people assuming that the process is the problem. How can this be avoided in a data warehouse environment? The keyword here is data cleansing, and building up-front verification procedures to prevent receiving inaccurate data from outside sources.

Insufficient Network Capacity

A businessperson's general knowledge of network capacity should consist of the following:

- Traffic

- Rate

- Time

Traffic is the amount of information being transferred. Rate is the speed at which information is moving. Time is how long it takes to get the information you need once all the parameters have been entered. You do not need to know anymore that those three items. The network people will provide the rest. However, you will need to give them an estimate of how many people will be using the system, the type of information that will be requested (a.k.a. type of queries), and the response time (tolerance) required (for example, once the parameters are entered the user will require a two-second response). Be very careful as to the information you supply the network people with. If you underestimate, your system will experience time delays. It will not matter that your data warehouse contains the most accurate information in the world. If the system cannot deliver it within a reasonable time, according to the work demand, nobody is going to use the data warehouse the way it was intended to be used.

One way to reduce the possibility of insufficient network capacity is to partition or slice the data warehouse at the location that it is really needed. This would be based on specific or general data requirements for each user location.

All or Nothing

When starting a data warehouse project, people assume that the original list of requirements is the minimum expectations they are looking for when the project is implemented. However, in the real world, the project might not meet all of its original objectives in the first release because of time constraints, budget limitations, or weakness in skill levels. Building a data warehouse is similar to building a house. The architect will lay out the plans, but sometimes the desired material will not be available. It does not mean the house will not be built; it just means the house will be built a little differently than expected. The house will still provide basic functionality, and as time goes by, what was missing can be added. Data warehouses could be built the same way. There is a lot of compromising and workaround required. If you insist on everything following the original specifications exactly, you not only will be disappointed, you will have jeopardized the data warehouse's chances of meeting its other goals. In addition, it increases the risk of failure. Incremental implementation is the largest key to success for a data warehouse. On the other hand, if the primary objective of the data warehouse cannot be delivered, you have a problem.

One way that has been proven successful is to subsidize or partition the development of the data warehouse effort into business subject areas. This division will allow you to focus on one area of business. One critical concern when working in partitioned areas is that you forget the other areas. Make certain that you have completed the information architecture first. Otherwise most of your time will be spent cleansing the data from incorrectly defined business rules.

Unanticipated Growth

Successful data warehouse implementations create more demand than anticipated. Growth must be managed. The original plan must be reviewed and tweaked with each implementation to allow for adjustments in business needs. Business users can be added to the data warehouse:

- If the current network configuration can support the increased capacity and location

- If their needs can be satisfied with the current contents and tools of the data warehouse

- If they have or can obtain the proper training

Existing business users may request that additional information be stored in the data warehouse. If the analysis and design were done correctly, their request should already be part of future implementation plans. If it is not, the additional requirement must be analyzed as to its impact on the data warehouse's infrastructure. Major changes may not warrant the increased expense. It all comes down to the impact on the ROI and the executive sponsorship's agreement to the change.

Whenever possible, put the request for new users and requirements through the defined maintenance process.[11]

Summary

This chapter addressed the key areas that a business manager needs to be sensitive to before deciding to build a data warehouse. The main focus is to ensure that the reader has an understanding of what is being said and knows how to interpret the answers to your questions. The reader should understand the typical reasons for data warehouse successes and failures. You should be able to proceed with your data warehouse project with confidence because this chapter discussed key risks and how to avoid them.

The most important point to remember from this chapter is the knowledge contained in the business area, which should drive the data warehouse's success. Managing the project is a joint effort between business and information technology. However, business must continually be involved to ensure compliance to data warehouse requirements, goals, and objectives. The process is tied to management. Data warehousing requires following a mature process. A data warehouse is a complex technology. Following a formal process will reduce the risk of failure. Finally, the data warehouse is built upon both infrastructure and architecture. Keeping it simple and tied to the business objectives will enhance the data warehouse's success and longevity.

Each of the items discussed has a direct impact on the data warehouse's success. Ironically, none of them has anything to do with technological knowledge, but rather business knowledge, management, and communication.

To briefly summarize, remember these points:

- Clearly define requirements and maintain scope.

- Assign knowledgeable resources; details are important.

- Facilitate communication between the business units and information technology by using business terminology.

- Business is in control of the project. Manage the project for all incremental releases with a formal project plan.

- Keep quality and time in check. Monitor all deliverables and checkpoints.

- Employ easy-to-use tools whenever possible.

- Keep it simple (infrastructually and architecturally).

Refer to this chapter when you feel your project has lost direction, new personnel join the team, or simply when presenting the status of a data warehouse project. Have periodic checkpoints throughout the process to ensure that the project continues with its success. Recognize signs of possible causes for failure and use the techniques described in this chapter to correct the situation immediately. By using the techniques described in this chapter, you are on your way to implementing a successful data warehouse.

The objective is for the business manger to maintain control of this labor-intensive process. The goal is to implement a data warehouse that brings data to knowledgeable workers before the competition does. Chapter 4, "What Do I Do With It Now?" describes related information technology to facilitate access to the data.

4

What Do I Do With It Now?

C hapter 3, "Keys to a Successful Implementation," discusses techniques that a business manager can use to successfully implement a
data warehouse. This chapter concentrates on what happens after the
implementation, which will be divided into two sections:

Section One: After Implementation

Section Two: Integrating With Other Technologies

Section One: After Implementation discusses what a business manager can do to ensure a data warehouse's continued success until it
becomes obsolete. The business manager may not be the same person
who initiated the effort. However, it is important to understand that a
data warehouse can become a failure at any point in time. Therefore, it is
important for a business manager to remain involved throughout the life
of this mission-critical application. Maintaining a level of involvement
requires a business manager to continually review existing usage and to
be aware of new opportunities for growth. This section of the chapter provides the business manager with simple techniques for monitoring the
data warehouse throughout its life. The objective of the business manager
assigned to the task is to ensure that the data warehouse continues to
meet business objectives and maintains a positive ROI.

Section Two: Integrating With Other Technologies concentrates on the
integration of a data warehouse with other technologies that will
strengthen its use. These technologies can fall into two categories: data
access and data usage. Both technologies are required to facilitate a business manager's success. Some of the technologies are discussed with the
information technologist during the business case[1] (step 2) or designing

65

(step 4) steps of implementing a data warehouse.[2] Another scenario is to wait to implement these data warehouse enhancements until after initial implementation. Whichever scenario is used, these tools only become useful if a business manager knows what the users want the tool or technology to do and how to use them with a data warehouse. Therefore, the second section of this chapter concentrates on the integration of other technologies (including existing applications) with a data warehouse. Its purpose is to assist business managers in interpreting how to leverage these options by explaining the technology as it relates to data warehousing.

The Possibilities:
The Story of Fidelity Investments

Let us review a successful data warehouse implementation and the value it provides to the business community. One example of the endless opportunities and direct impact that a data warehouse can have on a business is shown by its implementation at Fidelity Investments. While reading this success story, think about what other technologies were implemented to facilitate access and usage and what the business manager must do to facilitate continued success.

Fidelity's data warehouse has grown to 500 gigabytes.[3] It is a data warehouse and not an on-line transactional system. However, million-dollar decisions are made that require up-to-the-minute information. Therefore, Fidelity's data warehouse is only fifteen minutes behind transactional trading systems. Controllers have the ability to view trading activity using many types of analysis techniques that evaluate risks and exposure at any given point in time. As a result, Fidelity is using the data warehouse to achieve its corporate goal: the continuous monitoring of operations, funds, risks, and exposures. The data warehouse satisfied this goal by extracting and cleaning data from multiple sources and providing consistent data across trading desks throughout the world.

Stories like the one at Fidelity and any other corporation currently using a data warehouse, would not have been possible without the business manager's involvement. The business manager's ability to assist with the analysis, design, and implementation of a data warehouse does not end there. The continued success of a data warehouse also depends on the business manager's level of involvement. Only the business community can alert the information technology organization of new requirements, new users, corrupted information, or performance (perceived or real) bottlenecks.

The success of Fidelity's data warehouse also involved selecting the correct data access and usage tools. Products are becoming available on a daily basis. It is difficult for technicians to keep abreast of the latest offerings, to differentiate between them, and to know how to integrate them into a total data warehousing solution for the business community. The business community must continually alert the information technicians of their data access and usage needs. By understanding the business's requirements, the technicians can continually review new tools that may better satisfy the business needs of the data warehouse. This includes:

- The ability to identify hidden business opportunities

- The ability to improve data quality

- The ability to obtain information more effectively

- The ability to improve decision making

- The ability to save time and money for the delivery of data-related decisions

The discussions in this section will be limited to technologies that affect the business community directly. Tools that enhance the design, development, and implementation of a data warehouse will not be discussed.[4] The technologies that are discussed include the business community in the decision to use and buy. Linking the technologies is the key to unlocking the full business intelligence potential of a business manager.

After Implementation

It is important for business managers to realize that their role is not finished after the first or final planned implementation. The business manager who initiates the effort is the data warehouse's business sponsor. This position comes with several responsibilities.

Business Data Warehouse Management

The business manager should be considered part of the data warehouse team but not part of the information technology organization. Business managers should be held responsible for the data warehouse's continual success. This can only be accomplished through frequent status meetings that review new requests from the business community as well as through monitoring the data warehouse's usage. It is up to a business manager to ensure that the data warehouse continues to benefit the corporation. Therefore, it is important to have an individual from the business community involved throughout the life of the data warehouse. The business manager's responsibilities include:

- Reviewing new requests from the business community

- Ensuring that business users are properly trained

- Ensuring that business users continue to have access to the most appropriate tools

- Reviewing performance and reliability so that they are within agreed upon acceptable limits

- Ensuring that the current data warehouse continues to support existing needs of the business community and the corporation

- Ensuring a continual positive ROI

- Applying pressure when information technologists need to react to any defects uncovered

- Reviewing access to security data

Continuous Monitoring

Tangible monitoring, such as reviewing performance and reliability, is executed by the system's software and reviewed by information technology personnel. However, the same two variables have an "intangible" monitoring activity. Intangible monitoring refers to the business community's perception of the data warehouse's success. If a business manager can not achieve the expected results, it is important for him or her as the project's sponsor to listen to all negative comments. The solution may require investigation by information technologists or additional training for the user in distress.

Growth Management

It is important for the business manager to realize that the initial implementation of the data warehouse is only the beginning. Once users are introduced to the data warehouse, new ideas for its expanded usage will begin to come out of the woodwork, which will impact on its infrastructure[5]. Employee enthusiasm and company needs will contribute to the data warehouse's success but will also become a maintenance nightmare if not planned correctly. It is up to the business manager to "manage growth." Review the business needs of all new requests. Evaluate their impact on the current infrastructure of the data warehouse. Determine if the business need is better satisfied:

- By "adding" to the current data warehouse

- Extrapolating from the existing data warehouse to the businessperson's local server or "data mart"

- Having the business partners go their separate ways and building a data mart that will specifically satisfy their business needs

The important thing in any of these scenarios is for the business manager to determine the best solution to the business problem that will be the most cost-effective for the corporation. This outcome can be accomplished with assistance from information technologists. Each scenario must be reviewed on a need-by-need basis to ensure that the decision does not turn the successful data warehouse into a failure.

Integrating With Other Technologies

Having the data available in the data warehouse is only the beginning. A substantial amount of data can be stored in a data warehouse, which data can become overwhelming to a novice business user. The business community must be able to:

- Find the data it needs quickly

- Have confidence that the data is accurate

- Manipulate the information easily

If any one of these factors is not to the business community's satisfaction, the data warehouse will fail.[6]

The data warehouse needs to be integrated with other technologies to be successful. It is important for the business manager to know about these technologies and how they are used with a data warehouse. These technologies can be subdivided into two separate categories:

1. Data usage

2. Data access

Data usage refers to the tools the business manager uses to interpret the data contained in the data warehouse. The data is of no value unless it can be used to identify business opportunities or financial warnings. Tools are required to assist the business manager in analyzing the data. The irony is that the tool selection, purchase, and training are a relatively small part of the entire data warehousing project. However, data usage tools provide most of the benefits of data warehousing to the business community.

> If you give users a printed report, they have an answer for the moment. When you provide them an effective query tool and access to a data warehouse, they will have insight for the future. [7]

Data access refers to transmission or distribution of data or the results of analysis to the business manager or clients. Data is information at rest. It sits and does nothing until it is retrieved. There are many new business opportunities for products and services due to the expanded telecommunication options. Therefore, it is important for the business manager to understand these options, which will spark innovative ideas about what to do with the data warehouse.

On-Line Analytical Processing

The ability to deliver data quickly depends upon the infrastructure of the data warehouse. Data accuracy depends upon the source, extraction, and cleansing methods applied during the development of the data warehouse. Being able to use and manipulate data is dependent upon end-user software tools, which constitute the largest category of software tools available for data warehousing. These software tools require evaluation by the business community as to their ease of use and functionality. Software tools for data warehouses are used in the plural sense. Multiple tools are required depending upon the expertise and needs of the business community. More than one hundred and fifty vendors offer tools that assist the business community retrieve and analyze the data found in the data warehouses. Unfortunately, no software tool can perform all functions for business users of varying levels of technical expertise.

Queries and Reports

A basic facility of tools is to allow business managers to initiate data-related queries to the data warehouse. The results of such queries can be formatted into predefined reports. Tools exist in the industry to support business managers with this basic task. The tools are executed at the business manager's workstation and the results are presented textually or graphically. The business manager can use these tools to navigate around the data warehouse without knowing any technological language.

Multidimensional Analysis

A data warehouse does not imply only two-dimensional analysis. Tools exist to create multidimensional views of the data. The objective is to dynamically create and display documents containing computed values, which allows a business manager to not only drill up and down but across dimensions. The key to its success is to provide the flexibility to subtotal facts and measures across a multiple number of dimensions, such as time, geography, and product. The result is a multidimensional cube of data at the business manager's disposal to analyze in whatever manner is required. This flexibility is important to the user because it allows him or her to dynamically define the subtotal calculations. Vendor products vary greatly in the ability to accomplish this task.

Statistical Analysis

Statistical analysis includes basic functions such as averages or means. It also includes complex analysis such as regression, correlation, factor, and cluster analysis. Tools exist for the business manager to perform statistical analysis on the data contained in a data warehouse

Data Mining

Data is data. It is nothing if thought or interpretation is not applied to it. The amounts of data available to the business community is almost limitless. The goal of any business manager is to discover what the data is telling the corporation. However, discovery is difficult when the amount of data is too extensive for the average business manager. The vast amount of data becomes destructive when users attempt to achieve answers to difficult questions. As a result, the amount of information clutters the view to the extent that answers are no longer visible. Data mining automates the discovery process in a manner that is useful for determining trends and patterns in data. In other words, data mining assists in generating hypotheses. On-line analytical processing tools verify the data that supports the hypotheses. As a result, the two types of tools support each other.

Searching for answers by using multiple dimensions to uncover patterns in information can be difficult with simple inquiries. Software tools are available to assist the business manager in "mining" through all the available data. These data-mining software tools enable businesses and consumer marketers to improve distribution, specialize direct mail targets, and develop a new outlook on consumer behavior. Data mining differs from query and reporting tools since it uses statistical and analytical techniques such as neural networks, decision trees, statistical processing, and data visualization. These techniques exploit the information to get more value out of the data warehouse.

Query tools exist that enable the business manager to obtain specifics as to what is in the data warehouse, such as what the sales figures were by sales region for the last year. Data-mining tools take the inquiry one step further. Data mining attempts to uncover the significant factors involved in the fluctuation of sales. It attempts to discover relationships and hidden patterns that are not always obvious or known by the business manager. Inquiry or query-based tools require the business manager to understand the relationships of the data ahead of time.

Data mining is most commonly used by the business manager for the following:

- Trend analysis

- Direct marketing

- Fraud detection

- Forecasting

For trend analysis, data mining is helpful in identifying ways to reduce the cost or time-to-market. Data mining can also help in direct marketing to specifically identify the most desired customer. Fraud costs corporations billions of dollars a year. Data mining is used to assist businesses in identifying which occurrences are likely to be fraudulent. Predicting occurrences such as credit card purchases, cellular phone calls, or insurance claims that could be fraudulent provides information to the business community in time reduce their exposure. Forecasting is based upon neural networks. It learns from experience. It predicts outcomes by detecting patterns in data and making generalizations about it, such as identifying financial trends with stocks and asset allocation.

Data mining identifies the unknown via three approaches:

1. Classification studies (supervised learning)

2. Clustering studies (unsupervised learning)

3. Visualization studies

Classification attempts to forecast from historical data. Classification requires the business manager to direct the grouping of data results. This is accomplished by the following:

- The business manager defines the study or scope of a data-mining activity, such as predicting the number of employees who will leave the company next year.

- The study or scope requires a subject, which in this case is an employee.

- The term *supervised learning* requires the business manager to determine what is needed to define the subject (an employee). This results in building a model of the subject, which may include:

  —Employee number

  —Length of employment

  —Performance review

  —Job classification

  —Raise trends over the life of employment

  —If the employee is still employed by this company

  —If the employee likely to remain employed over the next one, two, or three years

Calculations are provided to determine the value for missing or derived fields (such as if the employee is likely to remain employed).

Data mining mines through the data to fulfill the model. The data collected is grouped or classified given the rules defined in the model.

Clustering or segmentation looks for similarities and differences that exist in the model. This is accomplished by grouping rows of data that share similar trends and patterns. It is unsupervised learning because the business manager does not have to identify a specific trait. With clustering, the business manager identifies segmentation or natural groupings. The number of groupings varies according to the business problem. This technique is typically used for affinity analysis to determine which items and categories are most commonly influenced by the data.

Visualization studies graphically present data. Thus, these studies visually display points that would normally not be identified in a textual format. By using visualization studies, businesses can identify the best location for a new store or where to market a new product or service. Excel is one example of two-dimensional visualization. However, more sophisticated tools can provide graphical views of three or four dimensions of data.

Although data-mining tools are growing in popularity, they are still in their infancy. However, in addition to the new products entering the market, existing products are being released with new and improved functions. The key to using these tools successfully is to understand the types of problems that data mining will help solve.

Current data-mining tools address a wide range of applications and business problems. The next wave of data-mining tools will be more specialized and allow customization for particular business problems. The objective is to build knowledge into a tool that support a specific business subject, such as credit risk analysis or house-holding for direct mailings. The business subject may also be specialized to support a specific industry, such as medical or financial. Therefore, data-mining tools of the future will either be general or horizontal business solutions or specialized vertical business solutions.

Client/Server Implementation

Client/server technology is a physical architecture. It can be implemented in a two or n-tier environment.[8] The purpose is to separate data acquisition, data access, and data manipulation processing functions among levels or layers of the technological platform. This separation enables the technician to take advantage of the hardware capabilities with respect to performance and security. Most data warehouses today are implemented using client/server technology. The decision to do so will be made by the technicians. The business manager has input into what functionality and data is to reside at which business location. This decision impacts on the infrastructure of the data warehouse solution.

Client/server technology is ideal for local access to the data warehouse within a single company. However, if the business strategy is to share data across multiple locations and corporations, other technologies may be more cost-effective and feasible.

Reaching the Outside World, Telecommunications and the Data Warehouse

Implementing a data warehouse provides a pool of data that will leverage intellectual capital in the organization. However, the data warehouse is the pool. Access to the pool is another issue that can be resolved using other current trends in technology.

Electronic Data Interchange

Electronic data interchange (EDI) is a means of electronically communicating between distinct corporations. The communication link is predefined between multiple organizations. The format of the data being transferred is also predefined. It is not a mechanism for ad hoc inquiries. However, it is a mechanism:

- For transmitting information that will populate a data warehouse

- For transmitting results of a predefined inquiry

What EDI provides is secure and reliable transmission of data between specific organizations in a predefined format and time. Combining the EDI facility with a data warehouse provides a means of communicating analytical results securely between organizations. The telecommunication facilities established to support the EDI transaction are generally more reliable than Internet facilities.

Extranet, Intranet, and Internet Opportunities

Whether access to a data warehouse is via Extranet, Intranet, or Internet, it is the wave of the future. Data is too valuable not to be shared. The marriage between the World Wide Web (www) and data warehouses serves the common goal of data access. Data stored in a data warehouse is useless unless it can be accessed by users when and where they need it. The web provides an inexpensive method to deliver information. Web development tools automatically link web pages to data warehouse applications. Web browsers are becoming a primary vehicle for access to data warehousing applications.

The Internet's growth is due primarily to the popularity of the web. The point-and-click access provides an easy-to-use access mechanism to data warehouse applications regardless of the underlying technological platform. It is an inexpensive data access method with a universal interface. The training is minimal for the business community. At an increasingly rapid pace, corporations are running part of their business through web browsers.

The "Internet" is a generic term for three different subsets. For the purposes of this book, Internet represents all three types. However, it is important to understand the distinction among the three types in determining the scope of data warehouse applications. The three subsets are:

1. Internet

2. Intranet

3. Extranet

Intranet is the term for a company-wide "Internet." Only employees, and possibly consultants, have access to this "private" Intranet. It is internal to the organization and is typically used for e-mail or conveying company policies and benefits applications. Extranet expands beyond one corporation. However, it represents an agreement by multiple companies to participate on the same "Internet." An example would be sharing data among state and local police departments or hospitals. It is still a private use of the web. Internet is global access by one and all. It is typically used for customer service and applications for sales, marketing, or advertising.

In the future, the Internet will be able to access not only data warehouses but the software tools that access these data warehouses. It may no longer be necessary to have these software tools on your personal computer. Instead, a user would access a web site for the data he or she needs and select the correct tool to use depending upon analysis requirements.

The beauty of the Internet is its ability to combine its own technology with that of the data warehouse as well as with the on-line analytical process tools mentioned previously. The value added by the Internet is the ability to provide a browser and search engines. The deployment is similar to any client/server deployment strategy. The question is: How many users will require access to the data warehouse at a given point in time?

A good example of this combined technology is the business markets division of AT&T. They combined data warehouse and Internet technologies to deliver customer information as well as sales and marketing data to a large geographically dispersed sales force. They were able to cut the delivery time of this time-sensitive information to one-fourth the time of conventional methods. Since the sales force already had direct access to the web, the additional cost outlay of this project was *zero* dollars.

Merging the Internet with on-line analytical processing is the next logical step. The complexity of this merger depends upon business need. The most common use of three-way combined technologies is the distribution of static reports produced from predefined, time-initiated inquiries. The Internet provides the most efficient way to distribute the widely needed analysis. An example of a more complex use of three-tier technology would be using the Internet to:

- Download on-line analytical processor (OLAP) software.
- Submit inquiries directly to mine the data warehouse.
- Receive graphical results.
- Feed workstation applications.

Due to possible network bottlenecks, more hardware and the subdivision of functionality and data will be required. This process will entail three- or four-tier technical architecture.[9]

Mobile Computing

One can not talk about the Internet without talking about the other phenomenon that is growing in popularity and demand—mobile computing. Your electronic organizer can be synchronized with data kept on your desktop computer at the office via a cellular telephone. Some of the technology is currently available. A salesperson can connect his or her laptop via a telephone connection and log directly into the home office's data warehouse. From a client's site, the salesperson can submit a query to calculate a portfolio with up-to-the-minute stock prices. Insurance illustrations no longer need to be developed from static data but can now use up-to-date information contained at the home office.

Integrating With Existing Applications

If the business community is already getting valuable reports from other systems, it might be worth the investment of modifying those applications to work directly with the data warehouse data. The information technologist will be able to review the impact on these applications. The changes may be as minimal as changing the source from the legacy database to the new data warehouse. However, the changes could be so significant that a total rewrite of functionality would be required. In the last scenario, a business decision will need to be made to determine:

- If the report is still of value and required by the business

- If the business need for the report justifies the rewrite

- If the implemented data warehouse can support the business need

- If the business can settle with the data on the report in its current legacy and possible corrupted form

What is important is to ensure that the business community requesting the report continues to receive the information in some form or another.

Object-Oriented Applications

There is a great deal of hype and reality about object-oriented applications. It is beyond what a business manager sees on a screen. It is the way applications are developed. Object-oriented is a different approach to analyzing, design, and developing applications. Object-oriented techniques may prove valuable in gathering and analyzing business requirements. Tools may be purchased that were developed using object-oriented approaches. However, databases that contain objects versus data are still in their infancy. Therefore, building a warehouse to store "objects" is risky. However, object-oriented applications can interface directly with relational or multidimensional databases. As far as business users are concerned, a tool or application that is object-oriented has little or no value to the business community. It is more important that the application or tool perform specific functions or support the specific data types needed by the business community.

Leveraging Microsoft Office Suite

Microsoft is a multibillion-dollar company that produces software to work on personal computers. Its products range from word processing to spreadsheets and have changed the way most corporations conduct business. In fact, many corporations have made Microsoft the standard for personal computer software. Therefore, it is imperative that the data warehouse, and its front-end access tools, be able to interface with Microsoft software. For example, data warehouse inquiries should produce output, or create files, that can be read by any of the following desktop tools:

- Excel[10]

- Word

- Access

- PowerPoint

This may seem to be a trivial point. However, most business managers use the above products to produce reports for executives. The key is to have a minimal amount of manual manipulation by the business user. Manual manipulation can result in missed typing errors as well as the waste of valuable time. It erodes at the ROI that a data warehouse can provide.

The Microsoft suite of products most commonly used to interface with data warehouses is Excel.[11] Excel can be programmed to receive data on file and disperse it into multiple sheets. Excel illustrates data results in a two-dimensional view. However, it displays textual, tabular results in a wide variety of charts (such as pie, line, or histogram).

Multimedia

Data comes in multiple formats: text, voice, diagrams, and multimedia images. Text is the most common data-type that is stored in data warehouses. Data warehouses are evolving to support complex nontraditional data-types such as voice and multimedia images. As a result, data warehouses currently support all types of data and analytical analysis. An example of a data warehouse application that involves a cross section of data-types is the use of voice recognition or image comparison to identify fraudulent individuals who have police records. Analysis can be done on a variety of ancient maps. All require a mixed-data–type data warehouse and on-line analytical processing tools, including visualization tools, that support multimedia data-types.

Summary

At the beginning of information technology's development, the need was to have systems gather data. Over the next forty years, the direction of information technology's growth and that need have changed. The need now is to transform data into information that drives a business. A data warehouse satisfies that need. However, it is a stand-alone type of storage for corporate data. A data warehouse is successful if the corporation can make better decisions, save money, increase revenues, and operate more efficiently. In order to accomplish this, user-friendly tools, such as software that supports data access, reporting, and business analysis, need to be purchased to make the data warehouse useful to the business manager and the executives. This chapter reviewed the more common technologies for these software tools that work with the data warehouse, thus providing the business manager with an understanding of which vendor tools need to be investigated and incorporated into the business case. How to assemble all this information into a winning business case is described in Chapter 5, "How to Write a Winning Business Case."

5

How to Write a Winning Business Case

Developing a data warehouse may be the best thing for the corporation. However, unless executive management understands and agrees with your opinions, the project will not be allocated the appropriate funding and resources required to implement one. Attempts to implement a data warehouse without sufficient funding and resources are destined for failure.[1] To obtain the appropriate support, the initiator of the project should develop a comprehensive business case with the assistance of information technology specialists. It is important for any information technology project to have a business case, and preparing one for a data warehouse is no exception. Therefore, a business case is the first and most crucial document a business representative will produce for a data warehouse project. The goal of this chapter is to explain how to write a winning business case for a data warehouse. Presenting the business case will be covered in Chapter 6, "Selling the Winning Business Case".

A business case contains the justification for the time and expense that the project will incur. The justification must clearly describe the project's scope, benefits, costs, and schedule. By reviewing the business case, executive management will be able to determine need and business impact by evaluating the ROI. In other words, the business case will be the selling vehicle for the data warehouse. Care must be taken to develop a business case that clearly and concisely illustrates why the business must have a data warehouse to survive. If it is written in a less forceful tone, the project will not be approved.[2]

The information contained in a business case for a data warehouse should be documented in detail to provide executive management with sufficient information to approve funding and to make the project a high priority. Due to the wide audience, the business case must be written in a manner in which every reader will understand and agree with the business need. A well-defined business justification will make the project a high priority and apply pressure on information technologists to implement the requirements as stated in spite of pressures from other time-critical projects.[3]

There is another motive for writing a clear and comprehensive business case. Once approved, the business case serves as the contract between business interests and information technology. The project's scope is clearly defined along with its control mechanisms. The control mechanisms, such as the project's plan or team roles and responsibilities, prevent runaway[4] information technology projects. By defining the project's control mechanisms, control of the project is placed in the hands of the business representative who initiated the project. Defining the scope of the investigation prevents information technologists from delivering what they think the business requires instead of what it really needs. Since information technology specialists assist in developing the business case, they have already agreed to the terms. With the business case details, everyone understands his or her role and responsibilities, and the time frame in which to deliver key milestones. At each milestone, the corporation will be able to tell if the project is still on track by comparing the actual to the proposed milestones. In basic terms, a well-written business case makes information technology accountable to the business.

Each corporation has a slightly different format for what should be contained in a business case. The purpose of this chapter and Chapter 6, "Selling the Winning Business Case," is to assist the business representative in developing one for a data warehouse project. Using the format described in this chapter will satisfy most corporate standards. If followed, the business case will be presented in a manner that will enhance the probability that it will be approved by the executive decision makers and it will serve as the information technology contract. By following these guidelines, the business representative will be able to organize important information so that it can be easily interpreted by executives. The result will be a comprehensive business case that ensures proper executive backing and information technology support.

A great deal of information must be gathered to write a comprehensive business case. This chapter will discuss what information is needed, where to research answers, and who will be responsible for gathering the details. This chapter will also explain each piece of information contained in any comprehensive business case. For the purposes of this book, each piece of the business case will contain a data warehouse example. Actual costs will not be provided since costs vary greatly between data warehouse business cases. Instead, this chapter will concentrate on the variables that make up cost estimates and provide guidelines for developing first-cut estimates. The variables will be categorized as infrastructural, architectural, and development/maintenance costs. Each category will be explained in detail to enable the reader to itemize the costs that pertain to their specific data warehouse business case.

The chapter is organized in a step-by-step format beginning with ways to convince management of the need for a data warehouse. This step-by-step format is:

Step 1: Convincing your manager

Step 2: Eliciting the assistance of information technologists

Step 3: Gathering the details of what and why

Step 4: Determining tangible costs

Step 5: Selling your idea (Chapter 6, "Selling the Winning Business Case")

Step 6: Plan B, if necessary (Chapter 6, "Selling the Winning Business Case")

Given the amount of information required to assist you in writing a winning business case, the last two steps, selling the idea with alternatives, will be covered in the next chapter.

Step 1: Convincing Your Manager

If you walk into your manager's office and state that the corporation needs a data warehouse to survive, your advice will probably not be accepted graciously. You will probably get a flat answer of no, or told to check it out after hours (while being assigned additional work).

Never walk into your manager's office without being prepared. Have some idea of what you want from the data warehouse that will entice your direct manager to allow you to investigate this option further. Be able to explain on one sheet of paper[5] what a data warehouse is, what it will do, and how it will benefit the corporation. State that all you want to do is *investigate* the possibility with the assistance of information technologists. Let your manager understand that after you build a business case, he or she will determine if it should be presented to the executive management committee.

Remember, keep it simple. Anticipate that you will probably have only fifteen minutes of your manager's time. Organize a one-page memo in a format that your manager will be able to read and understand while standing up on a crowded subway. If your manager prefers, use bullets instead of narrative.[6] Figure 5-1 (a & b) provides an example for a marketing analysis benefit. The first version is in narrative format, the second version uses bullets.

Describe what is contained in the memo, what you need your manager to do, and that you are available at his or her convenience to discuss this opportunity further.

When describing how the data warehouse will benefit the organization, pick a sore point for your department. Do not take this opportunity to define a goal for the entire corporation. You need to get over this obstacle first.

Step 2: Eliciting the Assistance of Information Technologists

A well-written business case will require the assistance of information technology. They will be responsible for providing approximately 75 percent of the information and can assist the business representative with developing the remaining portion. This section discusses how to initiate the data warehouse project with information technologists, what the initiator should have completed beforehand, and who to contact within the information technology department. This section also discusses exactly who should be involved from the information technology area to assist with developing a data warehouse business case.

The Information Technology Request

Gathering detailed information for a business case requires cost and scope information not readily available to the business community. Much of the cost information contained in the business case must be gathered with the assistance of specialists from the information technology area.

Figure 5-1a. Sample memo for a data warehouse investigation request (narrative).

MEMO TO: <manager's name>

MEMO FROM: <your name>

RE: Investigating the use of technology to shorten and enhance our current market research process.

1. *Current Situation:* <a short paragraph describing the situation>
Currently we use an outside research organization to provide us with key demographic data about our products and competing brands. The process takes approximately one month from the initial request to obtaining a printed report. The information is then keyed into our spreadsheets, along with additional data obtained from multiple sources within the company.

2. *Proposed Technological Solution:* <a short paragraph explaining how a data warehouse will improve the situation.>
We anticipate that we will be able to shorten the cycle of market research by having a direct access to a central source of corporate information merged with electronic feeds from outside market research organizations. The technology to be investigated for this merged, single source of marketing data will be a data warehouse. It will eliminate rekeying of data, obtaining conflicting data from corporate sources, and reduce the time to produce the marketing analysis.

3. Proposed Plan of Action: <a brief paragraph explaining your plans.>
I would like to spend the next two months, taking approximately 25 percent of my time, determining the feasibility of building a data warehouse to support the market research organization. With the assistance of information technologists I will identify the benefits and costs to the corporation of this approach.

Figure 5-1b. Sample memo for a data warehouse investigation request (bullet).

MEMO TO: <manager's name>

MEMO FROM: <your name>

RE: Investigating the use of technology to shorten and enhance our current market research process.

1 *Current Situation:* <two or three bullets describing the situation>
   • Outside research firms cost $$$,$$$ monthly and delays the analytical process by ddd days.

   • Rekeying of obtained paper format information into multiple spreadsheets adds ddd to the process.

   • Identifying correct figures to use for analysis when different answers are received from multiple sources delays process by ddd.

2. *Proposed Technological Solution:* <two or three bullets explaining how a Data Warehouse will improve the situation.>
   • Merge existing information with monthly general figure feeds from multiple research facilities.

3. *Proposed Plan of Action:* <list your plans in three to four steps.>
   • Define the scope with the assistance of information technologists.

   • Determine how much and how long it will take to implement.

   • Determine the ROI to the business for management review.

   • Develop a business case report and presentation with your approval.

The assistance of information technology is elicited by issuing an information technology request.

Many requests are received by the information technology organization. Requests without executive approval tend to receive a low priority status if left to information technologists. Therefore, it is important to write a request that captures the imagination and interest of the information technology manager. To do this, you must be prepared ahead of time. Have some idea what you are asking for by understanding the business implications of implementing a data warehouse. In other words, have an idea of what information you want in the data warehouse and what type of research the data warehouse will help you accomplish. Have more ideas than what is presented on paper to your manager. This will keep the conversation going and allow your manager to provide a few ideas that he or she does not see on the request. When your manager can provide additional uses, he or she becomes more interested in the success of the project.

This does not mean that you must know all your requirements. Specialized assistance from information technologists will assist you in identifying the boundary of investigation that will encompass a majority of the requirements. This is the "scoping" phase; your requirements are not carved in stone without opportunity for change. Requirements can and will be altered or added up to the point of implementation, with implications. It is the decision of the business area whether the impact is acceptable.

Data warehousing is currently a hot topic. A hot topic is either a new technology or new approach to development. It involves new tools that the technicians can learn. Technicians of all types love to work on new developments that require new technologies. It keeps them marketable as well as interested. Since data warehousing is a hot topic, getting assistance from information technologists may be relatively easy.

Remember, issuing a formal request for services is also a control mechanism. Information technologists tend to run and develop grandiose systems that do not satisfy business requirements when and if they are implemented. To prevent this from happening, follow a simple procedure of formality. Initiate the request for assistance in writing. From the start, show that you are the controller as well as the sponsor of the project. This is done by issuing a request for assistance to your information technology contact.[7] Figure 5-2 is a template that can be used for this purpose.

Formal information technology organizations require a formal request before any assistance is provided. Its purpose is for the project

Figure 5-2. Information technology request for a data warehouse.

Issued:	\<Date\>
Requested by:	\<Name of the Business Sponsor\> \<Department\> \<Telephone Number & Electronic Mail Address\>
Request sent to:	\<Name of the Information Technology Contact\> \<Department\> \<Telephone Number & Electronic Mail Address\>
Subject:	Data Warehouse Business Case

This is a request to discuss a possible data warehouse solution for *\<mention the business units that will be involved\>*. I would like to arrange a meeting with the appropriate information technologists to assist in clearly defining the business case. The goal of the business case is to obtain executive management's approval and funding for implementing a data warehouse. The target date to present the business case to executive management is *\<date two months out\>*.

Overview of Request:
   \<A short paragraph describing the request. Briefly describe the type of information you want to keep in the data warehousee. Include the type of research the data warehouse will serve.\>

Business Opportunity:
   \<A short paragraph describing the business opportunity. Briefly explain why the business needs a data warehouse. Include topics such as increasing market share or identifying cost saving opportunities. Include a minimum of three.\>

Current Situation Weaknesses:
   \<A short paragraph describing any weaknesses in current technology, systems, or manual work flow that would be improved by implementing a data warehouse. State time lost due to the manipulation of information in its current format to obtain critical information.\>

Impact to the Business if Project Is NOT Approved:
   \<An itemized list of what might occur, such as missed business opportunities, if the project is not implemented. Mention the possibility of a competitive advantage that other corporations have by using this technology.\>

Constraints this Project Must Work Under:
   \<A list of any constraints (such as budget, business contact availability, or time) that this project must work within. Make a specific note as to when you plan to present the business case to executive management.\>

---

leader or manager to allocate appropriate resources and time. This procedure is very common for organizations that have charge back facilities.[8] Even if your organization does not require a formal request for services, it is a good idea to write one. As stated previously, a written request shows information technologists the seriousness of your request and who is in control.

Concentrate your efforts on business justification. Information technology groups are and always will be cost conscious. Detail provided in these sections will enhance the probability of obtaining immediate attention. Besides, this information will eventually be the driving force in the business case for a data warehouse.

The Specialists

Many individuals will assist in the planning, designing, development, and implementation of the data warehouse.[9] When developing a business case, there are three individuals from the information technology area that you should be able to call upon for assistance: the project leader or manager, a data analyst, and a business information analyst.

A project leader or manager is the technology person who leads and controls the data warehouse project. In many organizations, the project leader or manager is responsible for all projects within a specific business unit. If this is the scenario in your corporation, it is recommended that you bring this contact into the loop as soon as possible. This person will assist you in obtaining specialized technological resources that are needed for developing a data warehouse business case. He or she will arrange all contacts with specific data warehouse vendors. The project leader or manager will assist in identifying all variables associated with costs. This person's responsibilities for developing the business case are:

- Determining development time

- Identifying the number of resources

- Identifying hardware and software to investigate

- Estimating all technology-related costs

The next person to be assigned from within the information technology area is a data analyst[10] who will be responsible for analyzing the business's information requirements at project, department, and corporate level. Data analysts are trained to assist the business representative in identifying information requirements that enhance business. Data analysts will ask the business representative questions about what information is needed and how it will be used to identify the details and organization requirements for the data warehouse.

Do not attempt to implement a data warehouse of any size without the assistance of an experienced data analyst. Data warehousing is within the data analyst's domain. It is what they are trained to do. The mere mention of the possible implementation of a data warehouse will have them begging for participation. They define a data warehouse as a pool of business data captured and stored in a format that will be flexible and easily interpreted by the business community. Getting it to that point takes an experienced data analyst.

The data analyst's assistance in developing the business case will help to define:

- The number of subject areas within the scope

- The amount of information to be stored

- The impact of the different dimensions

- The data warehouse infrastructure

- The source of the information to populate the data warehouse

- How long it will take to cleanse the data[11]

- Different implementation strategies

- How long to implement each strategy

A business information analyst specializes in work flow or process (function or task) analysis. They analyze the business process flow to determine the ultimate use of processes to fulfill business requirements. On many projects, the person assigned as the business information analyst will also take on the role of spokesperson for the business representative. As a result, they usually remain with the project from inception to implementation, thus assuring that the business representative's needs and requirements are met. Business information analysts are good people with whom to stay in contact. They are a source of information on who, how, and why something is needed during the development process. They can also keep you posted on project status and when and how to intercept any smoke screens. For a data warehouse project, they may take a back seat to the data analyst. However, the business representative may want to have someone from the application area to assist with the project's progress, or as a second pair of eyes for interpreting the data warehouse blueprint, or for assistance in determining how to use one.

The business information analyst's assistance in developing the business case will help to:

- Define what questions the data warehouse must answer.

- Develop the selection criteria for hardware and software products.

- Keep the data analyst from overanalyzing.

- Keep the project within scope.

Step 3: Gathering the Details of What and Why

Many variables affect the cost and time of implementing a data warehouse. The purpose of this section is to assist the business representative in determining benefits and scope and documenting specific requirements for the data warehouse business case. All of this affects time and cost.

Tangible and Intangible Benefits

The business case must define the projected benefits and balance them against the associated costs and risks. Examples are provided in Chapter 4, "What Do I Do With It Now?" However, benefits are a crucial piece of information in the business case. Therefore, the most common benefits will be reexamined here in the context of explaining how to determine the costs and ROI.

There are two types of benefits: tangible and intangible. Tangible benefits are directly associated with monetary value. The business case will use the first five years of implementation as a benchmark with which to compare the actual results, costs, and benefits to assess the ultimate success of the project. If the proposed data warehouse incorporates multiple business areas, each area must be represented with a tangible benefit. It is desirable but not necessary to break down each benefit by the different business areas.

Every corporation should look at methods for reducing their operating expenses. Chapter 4, "What Do I Do With It Now?" provides many examples of how to do so. Identify tangible benefits that can be tied to that objective. Examples include eliminating the need to use outside research companies for analytical and statistical information, increasing savings by reducing duplication, cutting back on expenses, and outsourcing. A little thought often can result in substantial savings.[12] Most of the potential data warehouse information is probably managed within a word processing package or spreadsheet by someone within your organization. Identify the time savings of that manipulation.

Outsourcing is popular with many organizations. Research may be one of these outsourced areas. However, when attempting to be the first to market any new idea, it may be cost-effective to bring the base information in from an external source, such as a research company, but to analyze the information internally. The increased knowledge obtained from the analysis and the reduced amount of rework might pay for the data warehouse in its entirety. The increased data security of the analysis will prevent a competitor from feeding off your research.

Time-to-market is also very costly. Using the research firm again as an example, determine the savings of having the information immediately versus waiting for the delivery from the research company.

In addition to identifying the possible tangible benefits, determine the critical performance measures that define success for each business area; for example, sales require sales dollars and number of products sold.[13]

A global benefit to a data warehouse is the cleaning of existing information. How many times have you received multiple reports from different production systems with different values for the same thing? The data warehouse becomes the central source of all business information. No more backtracking to identify the differences in sales figures, employee statistics, or insurance claims. The time and money spent researching and analyzing could pay for the data warehouse.

The information is no longer two dimensional but can be viewed in multidimensional format. The data warehouse format can manipulate the information easier than reading multiple paper reports.

The physical architecture of a data warehouse can provide information to decentralized locations quicker and more accurately. For example, the data warehouse can provide global corporate information to individual sales locations via replication of information or distribution of a specific piece.

Tangible benefits can be tied to saving time. Apply appropriate employee costs for that saved time. Calculate that amount over a one-, two-, three-, four-, and five-year period. Remember to apply the differential of the cost of a dollar over the five-year time period.

In summary, the tangible benefits of building a data warehouse fall into the following categories:

- Labor costs of manipulating information from multiple sources
- Competitive advantage of being first-to-market
- Reducing time-to-market

- Analysis time of identifying the correct information from multiple sources

- Availability of analyzing the combination of corporate information with outside information in one location

- Reduced time to determine corporate critical performance criteria

- Quick access to global corporate information from individual sales locations

- Multiple manipulation patterns of data to uncover new information

Intangible benefits usually do not have an associated cost-savings. They typically relate to corporate morale, good will, or the ability to make a presence in a new market. Although they are an asset, intangible benefits should be kept to a minimum. Executives want to see costs versus revenue.

Defining the Scope

Before writing a business case, it is important to understand the scope of the investigation. This is probably the most important part of the entire development process. The scope will be the basis for determining the costs, feasibility, and implementation of time frames. It is important to not calculate costs and time frames without the assistance of information technology specialists. They have the skills to determine the scope and access to information to determine cost variables.

Again, defining the scope is the most crucial part of determining cost. It determines the amount of information you need to keep and the number of users who will be using the data warehouse. At this point of the project, you will not have all the detail needed to define the scope of the data warehouse.[14] However, you will have a basic understanding of what information you want to keep. A ballpark estimate of cost and development time can be applied to that basic understanding.

The scope will include:

- The number of business units the data warehouse will support for each implementation phase (for example, marketing is the first phase, human resources is the second phase).

- The number of "things" as far as the type of information each business unit wants to capture and analyze (for example, customer, product, and employee-type information).

- The dimension of the information (for example, product sales by month and by geographical region).

- The number of locations requiring access to the information (for example, each sales region must have access to their specific information).

- The distribution mechanism (for example, whether or not the information will be sliced and diced and distributed to individual sales regions).

- The number of business users who will have access to the data warehouse by implementation phase. This will minimize costs because it will prioritize and minimize what information must be available for each implementation phase. For example, phase one could be the sales data for the eastern region for new products only; estimated implementation time, one year.

- The number of different tools that will be used by the user community. If the tools are satisfying different requirements, it is recommended to minimally estimate two different tools as part of the cost estimate.

This information will be gathered from the targeted business units by the information technology specialists mentioned previously. Some of this information may be available from previous information technology implementations. It is important to remember that this is a ballpark estimate. Therefore, do not allow the information technologists to spend a great deal of time gathering this information. The business case should be developed within one month's time.

With the time and cost estimates derived by your information technologists in hand, begin calling business organizations to compare estimates. If it is not possible to contact specific organizations, contact data warehouse vendors as well as industry analysts[15] for their experience in this area. If possible, obtain actual cost versus the proposed cost. Make certain that you compare apples to apples by comparing:

- The size of their data warehouse

- New hardware and software purchases

- The number of users

- Implementation time for incremental phases

Document Specific Requirements

Business requirements[16] will probably not be completely uncovered when writing the business case. However, key requirements that will have a significant impact on the cost of implementing a data warehouse will be identified. Knowing what information and what to do with it is only part of the equation. Those variables affect the data warehouse infrastructure. Other factors that affect the cost of implementing a data warehouse fall into the architecture category.

Architecture

Architecture is the schema of the technical environment in which the data warehouse will operate, including what can be reused from the current environment. The architecture, developed by information technology specialists, will document the physical technical structure of the data warehouse. This includes identifying the physical hardware, system software, and networking communication requirements. This information will assist in determining the cost of new hardware, software, and network communication facilities. It will be dependent upon business requirements concerning:

- The different data warehouse access locations

- The volume of information needed at each location

- The level of expertise of the business community accessing the information

It is important to document the previous information in phases. Determine what architecture can be used or needs to be purchased for each incremental implementation.[17] It is also important to anticipate the need to support growth over the next five years. Many data warehouses fail to anticipate sharp growth spurts as they become known throughout the business community. Growth spurts stress all components of the technical architecture requiring upgrades and involve additional excessive costs.

Software

Dependent upon the answers to the previous three architectural questions (access location, volume of data, and level of experience), are the additional software needs to be purchased to satisfy each business location's data access requirements. The answers will identify the number of tools that may be required. Information technologists and the business community will jointly select the tools. Dependent upon the end-user data access requirements and level of expertise, purchase of end-user tools will be required to support:

- Predefined reporting

- Simple ad hoc queries

- On-line analytical queries

- Multidimensional investigation

- Mathematical or statistical analysis

Data warehouses are built upon existing sources of information. Whether the information is internal to the organization or purchased from an external source, the information needs to be extracted, transformed, and scrubbed[18] before being placed into the data warehouse. Tools do exist in the industry that assist with this time-consuming chore. Those tools will be selected by information technologists but must be included in the cost of implementing the data warehouse.

Add into the software equation the purchase any data from external sources. For example, you may wish to change your customer reference information to correlate to the Dun & Bradstreet industry format. You may wish to purchase actual sales statistics on a monthly basis from experts in your area to incorporate into your data warehouse. You may wish to purchase multiple industry projections to develop a probable average for your analysis. These costs are identified by the business area. Each may have a different requirement and require multiple feeds from external sources.

Hardware

Hardware includes the purchase of new personal computers, printers, and other peripherals. It also includes any network communication equipment between users of the data warehouse and the data warehouse engine. Storage must be included depending upon the architecture. Make a note of what existing equipment can be used. Break down the cost of new hardware with the time it is needed. Hardware may not have been selected at this point in writing a business case. However, technicians will be able to give you a ballpark estimate[19] based upon the data warehouse's architectural design and the answers to the architectural questions.

Step 4: Determine Tangible Costs

This section discusses how to transfer the requirements into costs. Gathering the details during step 3 introduced a discussion of the data warehouse's infrastructure and architectural implications. Additionally, other variables affecting those costs are usually forgotten during the writing of the business case. These are the implications of total product purchase, outsourcing development, and anticipated growth and maintenance. Each of these implications and their effect on the overall cost of implementing a data warehouse will be discussed separately.

Infrastructure and Architectural Costs

Costs vary from data warehouse to data warehouse. Final cost depends upon the ability to use existing equipment, the size of each incremental implementation, and the condition of existing information. Unfortunately, how much the data warehouse will cost is executive management's first question. At this stage, all you can give them is a ballpark figure that is dependent upon the infrastructure (scope) and the architectural (technical) design. Therefore, it is important to itemize the costs as much as possible over a five-year period. To soften the bottom-line numbers, associate costs to tangible benefits that clearly illustrate the increased ROI over the same period. Wherever possible, do not lump the cost into the first year. Pull in other business units to assist with paying for the data warehouse implementation.

The largest impact on cost is the development that, in turn, is impacted by the size of the data warehouse. Figure 5-3 illustrates the size components.

The number of business units affects the number of people who must be interviewed and who must agree to definitions of the information to be kept in the data warehouse. Each individual group will have a different perspective of what the data warehouse must include. Each individual group will have a different point of view as to the meaning of business

Figure 5-3. Sample guidelines for determining how big the data warehouse is.

SIZE COMPONENT	SMALL DATA MARTS	MEDIUM DATA MARTS	FULL BLOWN DATA WAREHOUSE
BUSINESS UNITS	1-3	3-5	>5
KEY BUSINESS SUBJECTS	10	25	50
DIMENSIONS	1-4	5-10	>10
HISTORICAL REQUIREMENTS	6 months	2 years	5 years
APPROXIMATE DATA STORAGE SIZE*	Megabytes	Gigabytes	Terabytes
USERS	<15	15-45	>45
NUMBER OF DATA ACCESS LOCATIONS	1-10	10-25	>25
END USER DATA ACCESS TOOLS	1-2	3-4	>4
CONVERSION SOURCE FILES	4	8	20
FULL-TIME STAFF	4-8	9-12	>12
WORK EFFORT (in months)	>9	9-18	>18

* Data storage capacity for data warehouses is measured in one of three units of computer memory. Units of measure are megabytes (MB), gigabytes (GB), or terabytes (TB). The abbreviations for storage are usually listed as a number and the type of unit of measure. Megabytes, abbreviated as MB, is equivalent to 1,048,576 bytes, which approximately equates to one personal computer diskette. Gigabytes, abbreviated as GB, is equal to 1000MB or 1,073,741,824 bytes (100 diskettes). Terabytes, abbreviated as TB, is equal to 1000GB or 1000000MB or 1,099,511,627,776 bytes (100,000 diskettes).

terms. It is the responsibility of the data analyst to clarify business definitions. It is the responsibility of the data warehouse's project sponsor to resolve any conflicts in business terms and definitions. Understand that the more business units that are involved, the longer it will take to investigate and eventually deliver the data warehouse. Both will affect the cost of implementing the data warehouse.

The number of key business subjects defines the scope of the investigation. Key business subjects vary by business unit and some overlapping will occur. For example, sales and marketing are two different business units. Both are interested in product sales. However, marketing is more concerned with trends between geographical areas. Sales may be more interested in product sales by employees. Therefore, the results would be four key business subjects to include in the data warehouse: product, sales, geographical areas, and employee. Each key business subject will require further analysis and breakdown. Therefore, key business subjects affect the amount of development time as well as the data warehouse's size.

The word *dimensions* has been mentioned a few times in this chapter. It is an extremely important concept since it applies to different ways of viewing information. The most common method is to view data results by geographical area, product or service, sales results and forecasts, or time. The dimensional view results in sorting or aggregating data as it relates to the specific view. A bidimensional view would be similar to a spreadsheet. An example of a bidimensional view of the data is providing sales figures with regions and time. The months or quarters would be column headings, and the regions would be the row headings. Add another dimension, such as product, and you would have a three-dimensional or multidimensional view. Increasing the number of different views, or dimensions, of data impacts on the size and organization of the information. Each point of the multidimensional grid requires a different aggregation of data to provide the information. To increase the speed of calculating the aggregation, data may need to be redundantly stored, thereby increasing the size of the data warehouse.

The historical requirements are how much information must be kept in the data warehouse. You may decide to keep one year of detailed information, and summary information for two years prior to the current year. Whatever the decision, it affects the size of the data warehouse as well as the development time for calculating any summary information.

It may not be possible to know the actual storage size at this point. However, you may have a ballpark idea as to how big the data warehouse may be. For example, all the existing information (sales and products) you need from your current production environment is only 50MB. Unfortunately, that only represents one month of data. The data warehouse will probably be in the same range multiplied by the historical requirements (18 months). Next multiply the number of dimensions ([50MB * 18 months] * 2 dimensions). This number will probably be larger than what is finally implemented.[20] However, it is better to overestimate the size of the data warehouse[21] for the business case.

The number of users affects development time for gathering, training, and architectural requirements. For the purposes of the business case, anticipate the worst case scenario. Anticipate that the users are new to data warehousing and will require a great deal of hand-holding during the implementation phase. Do not skimp on training![22] Identify the access patterns of each user. This information will help determine the traffic load on the network and the possible need to upgrade any hardware. The access patterns may show that the users access the information more frequently the first Friday of the month but not at all by month's end. For this scenario, upgrading the network may not be cost-justified for one day of user inconvenience.[23]

The number of data access locations can affect the cost and time to develop in multiple ways. First is the network access to the data warehouse. If there are no telecommunication facilities linking each location to the data warehouse, networking equipment must be purchased. The data access locations also affect the data warehouse's design. Information contained in the data warehouse may be accessed directly from the main source, replicated at each data access location, or segmented across each location. Each method of distributing the information contained in the data warehouse has a development cost implication.[24]

The number of end-users' tools refers to the number of different user tools. Each group of users may have special query requirements that require different tools. There is a range of tool functions. End-user tools fall into one of the following categories:

- Data access/query tools

- Report writers

- Multidimensional database management systems

- Advanced decision support tools

- Executive information systems

The number of data conversion files has a major impact on the data warehouse's size and the amount of time needed to implement it. First, one must identify the correct source. Multiple production files carry similar information. It takes time to correctly identify the source. Determining how clean the information is in the conversion source files is another time-consuming activity. There are software packages on the market that can assist the information technologist in cleaning the data.[25]

The number of full-time staff is a cost-associated variable for every organization. Each full-time employee multiplied by his or her work effort is the clearest tangible estimate. However, it is the most vulnerable variable since information technologists do not have a good handle on estimating development time. There are products and methods available that will assist in the planning effort.[26] It is recommended that the estimate be compared to other data warehouse implementations, either within your organization or with outside organizations.

Of the ten items listed in Figure 5-3, only six have an impact on the size of the data warehouse.

- Business units (5%)

- Key business subjects (20%)

- Dimensions (30%)

- Historical requirements (25%)

- Number of users (5%)

- Number of conversion source files (15%)

Each item affects the amount of information that the data warehouse will hold in multiple formats. Figure 5-4 illustrates which items affect the size of the data warehouse the most. As depicted, the size of the data warehouse impacts on the cost of implementing and maintaining one. With this in mind, make certain that your dimensions and historical requirements are cost justified. The key business subjects will be the best

Figure 5-4. Data warehouse size.

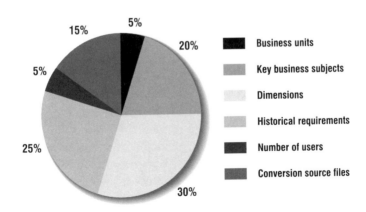

mechanism for subdividing the implementation. Leaving one key business subject until a later implementation will delay the dimensions and historical needs associated with it, thus, minimizing the size of the data warehouse over the five-year life of the project.

In summary, Figure 5-3 identifies variables that must be considered when determining the cost of implementing a data warehouse. The size of the data warehouse is not the largest cost item. However, size directly affects the most costly item in implementing a data warehouse . . . the development time. Development time and associated staff account for 50 percent of the implementation cost. Information technologists command a high price for developing a data warehouse. The larger the data warehouse, the more their time will be required. Of course, the better the individual, the higher the cost.[27] Figure 5-5 illustrates which items affect the cost of implementation the most. The variables affect cost in the following way:

Infrastructure (development time and cost):

- Number of business units

- Key business subjects

- Dimensions

- Historical requirements

- Conversion source files

Architecture (software and hardware):

- Number of data access locations

- Number of end-user data access tools

- Approximate data storage size

- Number of conversion source files

Some of this data may seem overwhelming to the business sponsor. Remember, the information technology specialists will assist in clarifying these costs. However, you may want to use Figure 5-6 to help identify other tangible cost items that need to be included in the business case. If possible, mention how the network and the purchase of hardware and software can also be used for other new or existing information technology projects.

Figure 5-5. Impact on data warehouse cost.

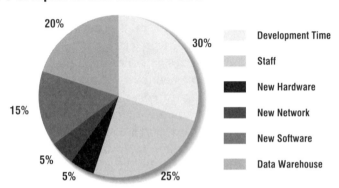

Figure 5-6. Sample tangible cost checklist.

COST ITEM	WHAT FALLS WITHIN THIS CATEGORY
HARDWARE	• Upgrade in central hardware • Additional new hardware • End-user personal computers • Color printers for analytical output
STORAGE	• Upgrade to central storage for data warehouse • File servers to hold distributed or replicated information (remember to include individual historical requirements)
PLATFORMS	• Wide-area network to hold distributed or replicated information • Middleware
NETWORK	• Communication equipment to the data warehouse • Number of locations requiring access
SOFTWARE & TOOLS	• Development • Analysis • Distribution and replication mechanism • Data extraction tools • Data cleaning • Conversion • Query (including data-mining tools)
TRAINING	• Data warehouse development • Tool usage • Data warehouse usage
HIDDEN CHARGES	• Organizational changes to support the new data warehouse

Product Purchase Implications

The business case should include any product that needs to be purchased to support the data warehouse. This might include a full architecture of hardware, networking communication, system software, and query software. The information you document in the scope section of the business case report will be the basis for writing a request for proposal that will be sent to potential vendors. A list of evaluation criteria, if known at this time, should be included as part of the scope. If you have not done so already, one of the milestones for the first stage is to develop evaluation criteria. The criteria should be developed with the assistance of the information technologists. There are approximately thirty data-mining vendors to choose from, and the list grows daily.[28] If you have identified a specific list of possible vendors, you may wish to include the product descriptions in an appendix for the business case.

Maintenance and Future Growth Considerations

The data warehouse is not complete even when the final incremental implementation is complete. New requirements and misunderstandings will be uncovered throughout the development effort. Each new requirement may be considered minor to the business area but may result in major conversions or enhancements to information technologists. Most misunderstandings should be caught before the final implementation; however, many misunderstandings result in defects[29] that can only be resolved by information technologists.

Future growth must be considered in the cost of building a data warehouse. Every successful data warehouse implementation involves new users and requests for more uses. People within the organization that you never heard of will be requesting access. This impacts hardware, software, and enhancement time.

In the case of new requirements, new users and uses, or defects, time and money must be allocated to the data warehouse project in addition to continued support from the information technology organization. Many business cases fail to alert executive management of this possibility. It will impact the ROI since you will not be able to itemize possible tangible benefits. However, you will not be asking for funding or resources until after the first incremental implementation. Therefore, the ROI will not be affected immediately. To obtain a ballpark estimate for maintenance and future growth, estimate the cost for a small data warehouse. Verify your figures with other data warehouse projects from other companies or industry specialists. Add a disclaimer similar to the one that is described in Figure 5-7.

Figure 5-7. Maintenance disclaimer.

The amount of $$$,$$$,$$$ for maintenance and enhancements has been included in the total cost of implementing a full data warehouse. This amount includes the resources and costs to support new users, new applications, and any defects uncovered during the implementation of the data warehouse. The costs include hardware, software, development, and training. This is a ballpark estimate in anticipation for the possible need for annual funding and resources to support the data warehouse. The request for this funding and resources will not be made until the success of the first incremental implementation of the data warehouse.

Summary

Implementing a data warehouse is a significant investment in time and money. However, the ROI can be realized by uncovering answers to difficult questions and being able to react to previously unknown findings.

To obtain the proper funding and resources for any information technology project, you must have the acceptance and support of executive management, which is obtained by writing and presenting a clear and concise business case. Writing a solid business case for a data warehouse is imperative. This chapter instructed the business executive or manager how gather the information for the business case (steps 1 through 4 of the business case process), and how to identify information that is difficult to obtain. This chapter discussed how to elicit the assistance of specific information technologists because a joint effort between business and information technology enhances the chances for success.

Once the data has been gathered, it is important to assemble the information in a format that will be easily read and interpreted by the busiest of executives. Chapter 6, "Selling the Winning Business Case," discusses the last two steps in the business case process. Chapter 6 discusses how to formulate, present, and sell a business case for a data warehouse project that will obtain the highest priority and funding from executive management.

6

Selling the Winning Business Case

This chapter continues the discussion of how to write and present a winning business case for implementing a data warehouse. As with Chapter 5, "How to Write a Winning Business Case," this chapter is also organized in a step-by-step format. This chapter begins with the development of the final presentation to obtain executive management's approval to take the next step in implementing a data warehouse. The full business case step-by-step format discussed in both chapters is:

Step 1: Convincing your manager

Step 2: Eliciting the assistance of information technology

Step 3: Gathering the details of what and why

Step 4: Determining tangible costs

Step 5: Selling your idea

Step 6: Plan B, if necessary

Steps 1 through 4 were covered in Chapter 5. However, writing the winning business case is only the first step toward obtaining funding. The written word needs to be followed up with a presentation to executive management. This involves a bit of selling. Therefore, this chapter discusses the final two steps of this process.

Step 5: Selling Your Idea

The person who initiates the data warehouse project ultimately becomes the project's sponsor. This individual is responsible for the project's success or failure. Once funding has been approved by the executive management committee, this person has the authority to decide how the funds are distributed, give the final word on requirements, and dictate how business resources are allocated. Therefore, this person should not only understand the company's strategic direction but also know the business community. It is the project's sponsor who must answer to the executive management committee.

Writing and presenting a business case is the vehicle to obtain proper funding and resources. Therefore, the business case involves selling the concept to key decision makers. This is accomplished with the written report and presentation. Remember the audience for both methods of communication. Although the same information is contained within each, the format must be tailored to the audience.

The trick to either format is to keep it clear and simple. Executives do not have time to read volumes of information nor to sit through endless presentations. However, building and implementing a data warehouse takes time and money beyond the average information technology system. Therefore, the facts must make the point quickly and clearly. Supportive detailed information must be easily accessible for detail-minded financial personnel. Therefore, put the detail at the end of the business case, in the appendix.

A successful business case ties the projects' benefits to the corporate goal. If possible, identify as the corporate goal a pet goal of the decision makers. Identify the weakness of the current situation in relation to satisfying that pet goal. When documenting tangible[1] benefits, the first item should relate to that pet goal.

Be assertive when expressing the costs of building a data warehouse. However, soften the costs by documenting them in three ways:

1. The overall cost with incremental implementations

2. The cost to ROI over a five-year period or for each increment

3. Step level approvals and funding for project continuance

The total cost of implementing a data warehouse is enough to prevent any decision maker from approving funding. It is a high-risk project based upon its cost, time to develop, and initially low ROI. Therefore, illustrate the costs by incremental implementation. The earliest increments should be tied directly to the key business area that will satisfy the corporate goal.

Each increment should illustrate a higher overall ROI. Include a line graph (five years by ROI percentage) that illustrates this point.

A data warehouse is a high-risk project. The successful implementation of data warehouses is equal to the number of failures. Decision makers want assurances about its success and the ability to apply some controls. The best way to satisfy this sense of uneasiness is to allow management the opportunity to cancel the project at the end of each step. (Of course, the reader will prevent that from happening by following the strategies in this book.) Using step levels of approval, funding and resources are budgeted only in small amounts at a time. By illustrating the controls and keeping executive management informed, the chances of the money running out will be minimal. This is just another way of providing a comfort level to the decision makers.

The Business Case Report

The business case report generally describes all the details gathered thus far, which are organized to paint a mental picture for executive management. The report will use the details gathered to describe:

- The current situation

- How it can be improved

- The benefits to improving the current situation

- The costs of improvement

- How the improvement will be implemented

Gathering details for a business case is a comprehensive, time-consuming task, but it is time well spent. It provides both the project's sponsor and the information technology staff an opportunity to identify the requirements for the data warehouse and to determine its benefits for the organization. However, gathering the details is only the first step. Assembling the information into a readable format for executive management is a major task. The information must be organized into a format that will clearly explain the benefits, costs, and project characteristics to obtain the appropriate approvals for funding and resources.

Every organization has its own specific format for a business case. Therefore, find a sample business case for comparison. The format that is described in this chapter is one that can be easily manipulated to match your corporate standards. If a sample business case is not available, the following format will probably be satisfactory.

The trick to formatting a successful business case is to organize the information in a top-down format. This requires making the point (executive summary), providing summarized information that supports the point (the body: where we are today, where we want to be, how we are going to get there), and providing details that support the summarized information (appendix). This top-down format targets all readers. Executives can obtain the concept of the request from the executive summary. The body of the document provides more information supporting the need for the request. The summary information describes the conclusions derived from the detailed research contained in the appendix. The appendix contains the details that were gathered from the information technologist's research. The research identifies how to arrive at the summarized conclusions.

The business case report should have an executive summary of no more than five pages, but preferably only two pages. It is a summary! It is enough information to entice the decision makers to read the more detailed body section, attend the presentation, and approve the project. Expanded narrative information should follow. This section should not be more than fifteen pages. This narrative expands on the itemized list contained in the executive summary. The detailed supporting material should be contained in the appendix. If it is a great deal of information, put it in a separate binder to be distributed only to those who request it (usually the financial officers).

The business case report is a compilation of your research. A sample business case table of contents is described in Figure 6-1.

Cover Page

Every document should have a cover page to inform readers about its contents and who to contact for questions. It should include the document name, authors with contact information, distribution list, and the date and time that it was issued and revised. Figure 6-2 illustrates what should be included. If the distribution list is too long, you may wish to add it as a separate page.

Executive Summary

This summary view allows executives to quickly read and understand the concept of the data warehouse project. This section is produced by the

Figure 6-1. Data warehouse business case table of contents.

1. Cover Page

2. Executive Summary

3. Document Purpose

4. Where We Are Today

5. Where We Want To Be

6. How Are We Going To Get There

7. Recommendations and Next Steps (Conclusion)

8. Appendix

Figure 6-2. Data warehouse business case cover page.

<COMPANY NAME>

Data Warehouse Business Case
for the <business area>

Contact Information:

  <Business sponsor's name>

  <Title>

  <Department>

  <Telephone number & electronic mail address>

Distribution List:

  <Name>

  <Title>

  <Department>

  <Telephone number & electronic mail address>

Issued: <Date>

Revised: <Date>

business representative, with assistance from the project leader or manager, business information analyst, and data analyst. Again, the executive summary should not be more than five pages (preferably two) and include the following information:

- A brief paragraph about the objective and purpose of the project

- The estimated tangible benefits

- The estimated cost to complete

- The estimated time to complete (broken out by each incremental or phase implementation)

- What must happen for the project to continue to the next phase

Figure 6-3 provides an example that can be used in any business case. Notice that by reading the executive summary, the decision makers understand what the project is about, why one is needed, and see the costs broken down into palatable pieces.

Figure 6-3. Data warehouse executive summary.

EXECUTIVE SUMMARY:
In the spirit of *<business goal>*, the *<department sponsored project>* proposes a return on investment of *<five year average ROI>* and a cost saving of *<total tangible benefit>* by implementing a data warehouse for *<business area>*. The data warehousing project will provide: *<list of top three to five objectives related to the business goal>*.

It is the objective of this business case to provide information to obtain executive approval and funding to begin this effort. Detailed supporting documentation follows the executive summary. To maintain the aggressive schedule, executive approval is required by mm/dd/yyyy* for $$$,$$$,$$$ to proceed to the next phase.

It is the understanding of the project team that the approval and funding are ONLY for the next phase of *<project name>*. Full commitment of funding will be requested at the completion of the analysis phase. The target date for the next executive management review is mm/yyyy *<two months out>*.

PROJECT OBJECTIVE:
A data warehouse is a repository of corporate information organized in a format that can be readily accessed and interpreted by business personnel. It is the objective of this project to design a data warehouse to support *<scope of the information and the research it will enable the business to accom­plish.>*

BUSINESS OPPORTUNITY:
   <A short paragraph describing the business opportunity. Why the business needs a data ware­house.>

IMPACT TO THE BUSINESS IF PROJECT NOT APPROVED:
<An itemized list of what might occur, such as missed business opportunities, if the project is not implemented.>

RETURN ON INVESTMENT (ROI): <add a chart>

Year	ROI	Tangible Benefit	Estimated Cost
Year One	##.##	$$$,$$$,$$$	$$$,$$$,$$$
Year Two	##.##	$$$,$$$,$$$	$$$,$$$,$$$
Year Three	##.##	$$$,$$$,$$$	$$$,$$$,$$$
Year Four	##.##	$$$,$$$,$$$	$$$,$$$,$$$
Year Five	##.##	$$$,$$$,$$$	$$$,$$$,$$$

CURRENT SITUATION WEAKNESSES:
<A short paragraph describing any weaknesses in current technology, systems, or manual work flow.>

TANGIBLE BENEFITS FOR IMPLEMENTING A DATA WAREHOUSE:
<An itemized list of tangible benefits with the associated cost savings.>

PROPOSED INCREMENTAL IMPLEMENTATION SCHEDULE AND IMPLEMENTATION COST:
Incremental Release 1 Implementation: mm/yyyy   **$$$,$$$,$$$,$$$**
<List Business Subject Area>

Incremental Release 2 Implementation: mm/yyyy   **$$$,$$$,$$$,$$$**
<List Business Subject Area>

ESTIMATED COST BREAKDOWN:
Incremental Release 1 Implementation: <add a chart>

	Analysis	Design	Construction	Test	Implementation
Hardware:	$$$,$$$,$$$	$$$,$$$,$$$	$$$,$$$,$$$	$$$,$$$,$$$	$$$,$$$,$$$
Software:	$$$,$$$,$$$	$$$,$$$,$$$	$$$,$$$,$$$	$$$,$$$,$$$	$$$,$$$,$$$
Development:	$$$,$$$,$$$	$$$,$$$,$$$	$$$,$$$,$$$	$$$,$$$,$$$	$$$,$$$,$$$
Training:	$$$,$$$,$$$	$$$,$$$,$$$	$$$,$$$,$$$	$$$,$$$,$$$	$$$,$$$,$$$

Incremental Release 2 Implementation: <add a chart>

	Analysis	Design	Construction	Test	Implementation
Hardware:	$$$,$$$,$$$	$$$,$$$,$$$	$$$,$$$,$$$	$$$,$$$,$$$	$$$,$$$,$$$
Software:	$$$,$$$,$$$	$$$,$$$,$$$	$$$,$$$,$$$	$$$,$$$,$$$	$$$,$$$,$$$
Development:	$$$,$$$,$$$	$$$,$$$,$$$	$$$,$$$,$$$	$$$,$$$,$$$	$$$,$$$,$$$
Training:	$$$,$$$,$$$	$$$,$$$,$$$	$$$,$$$,$$$	$$$,$$$,$$$	$$$,$$$,$$$

CONSTRAINTS THIS PROJECT MUST WORK UNDER:
<A list of any constraints, (such as budget, business personnel availability, time, use of existing networks) that this project must work within.>

*Due to the hardware and software implications of converting to the new millennium, it is strongly recommended to state all dates with a four-digit year.

The Document's Purpose

Although usually forgotten, it is important to include a standard paragraph describing the document's purpose. One never knows who will be reading the document. By omitting this paragraph, you risk that a new employee (decision maker) who is in charge of setting priorities and funding may not understand what and how to read this document. Providing a simple paragraph similar to Figure 6-4 reduces the risk. It is an example that can be used for any business case. The reason why it follows the executive summary is to minimize what the initial group of executives needs to read. They already know why they are receiving this document.

Figure 6-4. Business case report purpose.

The purpose of the Business Case Report to is to clearly define the business objectives for an information technology data warehouse project. The information contained in this document will provide the executive management committee with sufficient information to determine the priority for this project. This document defines the scope of the investigation and the next steps that will occur after receiving executive management approval and funding for project continuance. Project funding will be requested for the next phase prior to the completion of the current phase before continuance.

Where We Are Today

This section describes the state of affairs that currently exist. Stress both strengths and weaknesses. Wherever possible, stress tangible benefits with their associated costs as much as possible. For example, the amount of time spent rekeying information into multiple spreadsheets can be associated with the standard employee hourly rate.

Be very careful. Identifying weaknesses can be very political. Do not mention a weakness in a negative manner that was implemented by one of the key decision makers. Mention only those weaknesses that everyone can and will agree upon. These weaknesses must be accurate. Therefore, remove any opinions or emotionally charged statements.

Although you want to make a point, soften your analysis of the corporation's weaknesses. Discuss the benefits of correcting them and how the data warehouse will improve the situation. This would be a good opportunity, as an example, to mention how the outsourced research company has served a valuable purpose. However, by bringing the analytical work in-house, the data security would enhance the company's ability to bring new products to the market before competitors do.

No matter how bad you may feel about the current situation and how much you want to bring in a data warehouse, every situation has some strength to offer. Therefore, identify things that you do not want to change (especially if it is something a key decision maker sponsored). Identify how implementing a data warehouse will enhance what you do not want to change. Build upon the strengths of the company. For example, mention that the corporation analyzes its corporate financial data accurately. Implementing the data warehouse will enhance productivity by avoiding the percentage of time spent identifying the accurate (clean) data or reworking figure manipulation from spreadsheet to spreadsheet.

Where You Want to Be

Once you have defined the current situation, you can begin to describe the desired future. It is easier for management to understand the future and what a data warehouse will buy them once they have agreed upon the current state of affairs.

At this point, you paint a mental picture of what the data warehouse will do for the corporation. Be realistic. Do not oversell what a data warehouse will do for the corporation. Break it down into incremental achievements over a five-year period. Where possible, correlate these achievements to the weaknesses previously mentioned.

A data warehouse is a major investment in time and cost. Therefore, management will require progress reports. They want to know how your project will objectively measure success. The benefits you identify in this section will be what management will look for after implementation. Choose tangible and practical measurements. Tangible measurements would be milestone deliverables that are reached throughout the project's development and ROI figures over the next five years. Each milestone reached builds continued executive support and credibility for your efforts.

In outlining where you want to be, you must describe the boundaries of the data warehouse, also called the project's scope. This section discusses what the project will and will not include in the data warehouse by implementation phase. The project's scope is produced by the project sponsor, with assistance from the project manager or leader, business information analyst, and data analyst.[2] It is is a ballpark view and is not cast in stone. The scope will be finely defined during the next phase of the software development process.

1. *Dimension of scope.* A list of what is in or out of the scope of investigation. The deliverable may be in text or diagram format, or a combination of both. Include in the dimension:

- *Key business subjects.* List each subject with a definition; illustrate the relationships between all subjects.

- *Existing information.* The source of information to populate the data warehouse.

- *Dimension of views.* List each dimension with a definition.

- *Historical requirements.* Document how much detail you want to keep and why.

- *Data access locations.* List the geographical location of users who require access.

2. *New requirements.* A data warehouse consists mostly of existing information. However, this may be an opportunity to obtain access to outside information to incorporate into the data warehouse. This ability to access new outside information that the corporation does not currently have access to would be identified in the detailed list of new requirements.[3] For tracking purposes, each requirement should be itemized with an identifier, a short name, and a detailed description.

How Are You Going To Get There?

We are now at the development process of the data warehouse. The point of this section is to give executive management the impression that you are in control. How you are going to get there, or complete the project, adds credibility to the statements made in the previous sections. This is accomplished by defining a plan of action, project team, control procedures, assumptions, criteria for success, and project risks. This information assures executive management that the project and funding will be carefully monitored by you. Make it clear to the decision makers that executive management will be given regular feedback that they can compare to the business case. Depending upon the results of the comparison, executive management can award more funding or pull the plug and cut its losses.

It is not important for the executives to see every task or item. That detail will be in the appendix. Only the major milestones with their associated deliverables should be identified in this section. Phrase the listing in a language that the executive management committee can understand. Do not mention anything in information technology terms without a clear and concise definition. Remember, keeping it simple is best. Executives do not have time to interpret. It is preferable not to present anything that could be interpreted incorrectly. The result may be that your project does not obtain appropriate funding or resources.

Organize this section of the business case into the following:

- Project approach
- Project organization
- Training and support
- Assumptions
- Critical success factors
- Risks and countermeasures

Remember, all difficult assignments look doable in smaller pieces. Stress that you plan to follow W. Edwards Deming's[4] Quality approach: Plan, do, check, and act. This approach requires writing a detailed plan one stage at a time, acting upon the plan, checking the results with executive management, and obtaining approval for each stage. Finally, when acting on the approval to move forward, state exactly what executive management will approve at the next review.

Project approach describes the estimated project plan, which is produced by the project manager and includes a list of milestones, resources, requirements, and a schedule. An additional section should identify any assumptions that were made when creating the schedule, for example, the availability of resources or work completed by an outside organization.

- Phases
- Key milestones and their associated deliverables
- Implementation approach
- Resource requirements
- Project schedule summary

Realize that there is no way that you can completely estimate the entire project at this time. Instead, only estimate when the first milestone will be reached.[5] For a data warehouse, that would be the architecture diagram documenting all required information.

Project organization identifies both the business and information technology members of the project team. Specific resources may not be known at this point; however specific skills should be. You will know the role and responsibilities of each resource required. One of the key objectives of this business case is to obtain proper resources, which includes a key business resource for each of subject area. Included in this section are an organization chart, role definitions, and the responsibilities of the key business resource.

No project is successful without proper *training and support,* such as a description of any training requirements or outside support (operations, training, etc.) that will be required to implement the software product, which should be documented by the project manager.

Project controls should be completed by both the project manager and the business sponsor. This section can be broken down into the following format.

- *Quality Control Procedures* describe what controls will be in place to ensure quality.

- *Progress Control Procedures* describe the mechanism for keeping the project team (including business management) informed of status and issues.

- *Control Factors and Tolerance Parameters* describe the tolerance of what the business will accept in variation of the requirements. This may include budget, project delays, performance, and the amount of information available. The control factors describe how to control any variation outside the tolerance level.

- *Change Control Procedures* describe how to alert and document any changes to the scope of the project.

Assumptions refer to any criteria, facts, or conditions that the project plan is based upon. For a data warehouse, this might include using existing network communication facilities. No new locations will have access during the first implementation. It is extremely important to document any assistance from specific outside business organizations, such as an outside research firm, in this section. They may provide crucial data that needs to be imported into the data warehouse in a specific format.

Constraints are the documentation of any limitations and boundaries that the project must work within. For a data warehouse, the constraints might be to implement only a small data mart to prove the concept. Include a list of any constraints that must be considered when designing the system. Examples of constraints are:

- Implementation timing

- Budgetary

- Resource

- Existing equipment that must be supported

Critical success factors are key milestones that must be achieved for the project to be a success. Keep these milestones clear and concise. Make them as tangible as possible. Let management know, in occurrence order, what must be achieved. Management has an easier time dealing with smaller tangibles than big project intangibles. It is also easier to keep smaller pieces on track than big projects. Upper management can deal with itemized lists easier than a statement of goals. An example of a critical success factor for a data warehouse would be:

- The selection of end-user analytical tools within two months of the project's initiation

- The availability of key business personnel from each of the targeted business subject areas to be implemented

Building a data warehouse is a risky scenario. The failure rate of full implementation is high. Therefore, it is good to identify these *risks* directly with the executive management committee. However, no risk should be listed without an appropriate countermeasure. A countermeasure is the escape hatch if the risk occurs. Possible risks for implementing a data warehouse are documented in Figure 6-5.

Recommendations and Next Steps

A detailed business case helps build credibility. You are identifying what you want, why you want it, and how much it will cost and benefit the corporation.

Figure 6-5. Sample data warehouse risks and countermeasures.

RISK	RISK EXPLANATION	COUNTERMEASURE
Full implementation	Implementing a full data warehouse all at once.	The successful implementation of the full data warehouse will be accomplished in incremental stages. This will increase the time to implement the full data warehouse but will minimize the risk of it failing.
Loss of business support	Implementing the data warehouse will coincide with end-of-year processing. Access to the business community will be minimal during that time.	The project plan has taken into account the end-of-year processing. The project plan specifies the amount of business involvement and proper scheduling of the business users' time.
Network equipment delays	Networking equipment is backordered.	The first incremental implementation of the data warehouse will be to support the in-house business community only. Existing network communication will support these users.
Analytical software not working to specifications	Vendors of the analytical software demonstrated the workings of the product. However, the product may not work as demonstrated with the data warehouse architecture.	The product will be brought in-house for six months to test with the first incremental implementation. Payment for the product will be deferred until the completed test.
Not purchasing outside information in an electronic format	Eliminating the purchase of marketing information from XYZ Company in electronic format will prevent the business users from seeing the full market picture for product abc.	XYZ Company produces a paper version of the summary information. This information can be manually supplied to the data warehouse.

Conclude the report with a brief description of what happens next based upon approval to move forward with the project. This should include:

- What approvals are needed by management to continue with the project

- What will be done by the project team by the next management review

- When management can expect the next quality checkpoint review

The Appendixes

Appendix A: "Detailed Project Plan." A project plan depicting the estimated implementation plan. The next phase, documenting the business view (analysis) should have a detail estimate. All other phases would have a ballpark estimate. This estimate may not be clear to all who read this document. Therefore, it is important to have a disclaimer at the beginning of this appendix. Figure 6-6 can be used for this purpose.

Figure 6-6. Project plan disclaimer.

This project plan is a ballpark estimate based upon what is known about the request at this time. The plan will be adjusted as detailed understanding of the scope is uncovered. An updated project plan will be distributed at the end of each phase of development for the data warehouse. The next update will be provided to executive management <end date of the next phase>.

Appendix B: "Detailed Cost Justification." A cost-benefit justification analysis describing the added business value (tangible and intangible) upon implementing the software solution. This is a list of business reasons that support the implementation of the proposed project. Tangibles refer to items in the list that can have a cost saving or expense directly associated with it. The top-five tangible benefits are itemized in the executive summary. The appendix should contain all the supporting detail to back the top five and additional tangible benefits. Examples of tangible items are:

- Resource reductions

- Increased marketshare

- Reduced manual or automated processing time

- More accurate analysis

- Reduced cost of using outside sources for information

- Reduction in elapsed time between requests and delivery from outside firms

- Direct access to more information providing better analysis

- Access to more customers

Appendix C: "Detailed Risk Analysis." A cost analysis associated with the project's risks. Costs need to be associated to the countermeasures, a fact that is often overlooked by optimistic information technologists. However, it is extremely important for information technologists to understand the impact on the business of common unforeseen events[6] and to plan (countermeasure) if they occur. Sample risks would be:

- Loss of funding

- Hardware or software not working as anticipated

- Delay in project[7]

- Lost of project sponsor or other key resource due to organizational changes

The Business Case Presentation

The business case presentation should contain slides of the executive summary with bullets of information contained in the expanded narrative section. The presentation should never last more than one hour! Always make the decision makers comfortable, which means supplying coffee and food! Never arrange a presentation on a Monday morning or a Friday afternoon, or the day before or after a holiday or the decision maker's vacation. Make certain that all the decision makers, as well as the information technology executives, attend the meeting.

The recommended format for the presentation would be:

Slide 1. Cover page stating the name of the proposed project, and the date and time of the presentation.

Slide 2. The objective of the meeting (which is to obtain funding).

Slide 3. Weaknesses of the current situation.

Slide 4. What a data warehouse is.

Slide 5. The tangible benefits for implementing a data warehouse.

List each benefit with an explanation on a separate slide (limit the number of benefits to only three to five). Think about adding charts. One comparing the benefits to each other. Another comparing the benefits outweighing the costs.

Slide 6. The incremental implementation approach. State which business areas will be implemented when. Make sure that each business area that attends the presentation will be satisfied. Understand that this may bring some political infighting to be part of the first implementation. You may alleviate some of the politics by tying the incremental implementations to the corporate goals.

Slide 7. Costs, time frames, and ROI. This looks very good in a bar chart.

Slide 8. What is the impact to the business if this project is not approved. Add a chart illustrating projected gain (if the project is approved) versus what could happen with the status quo (if the project is not approved).

Slide 9. Next steps. This includes getting approval *for the next stage only.* A Gantt Chart can be effective for this slide. Explain what they will get for the money. State when you would like a decision by to keep the momentum of the project going.

Slide 10. Summary. (Remember, always thank the executives for their time and the information technologists for assisting with this business case.)

During the presentation of the business case, stress the key points three times! Remember Shakespeare's "Beware the Ides of March." Everyone who has watched or read *Julius Caesar* remembers the warning about March 15. It was mentioned three times during the play. Similarly, IBM training and presentation practice always follow a similar format:

1. Tell them what you are going to say.

2. Say it.

3. Tell them what you just said.

In other words, the key points that you want the audience (the decision makers) to remember must be mentioned three times! Use this trick to mention the one tangible benefit that affects ROI the most and you can be certain that you will achieve your goal. This will be the primary measurement of the project's success. It will be what the decision makers remember!

Obtaining Proper Funding

The track record that you and the information technology area have for deliverables will influence how easy it will be to obtain funding for this project. Keep in mind that you may have to account for a lame duck. If information technology is viewed as a cost-eating evil necessity that rarely delivers what it promises, then asking for funding will be much harder. Therefore, spend time with the information technologist and learn as much detail as possible before committing to any budget.

If your project must be presented to an executive management committee, here are some reasons why projects obtain funding and are given the highest priority:

- *Completeness of the project scope report.* This includes the level of detail identifying the investigation's scope and the business justification.

- *Clarity of the executive summary.* Executives are bottom-line–type people. They do not have time to read volumes of paper and interpret diagrams. Therefore, the project must be sold by the executive summary. It must entice them to read, or have someone else review, the details.

- *How closely it is tied to the business goals and objectives of the corporation.* Any cost expenditure must show just cause for proceeding with the project.

- *The more organized the project seems.* Organization provides a level of trust, leadership, and assurance that the expenditure will not be wasted.

- *Asking for commitment for the next phase only.* Management is willing to spend a little money to identify the feasibility of the project before committing to large expenditures for the entire project.

Step 6: When the Business Case Is Not Approved (Plan B, if Necessary)

There are circumstances where the project may not be approved even with a winning business case. Rejection does not imply that this is a closed issue. Where there is a will, there is a way. First find out the reason for the rejection. The reason may be one of the following:

- Fear of failure

- Lack of information technology funds

- Organizational control

If all the information described in this chapter was contained in the business case, then the most probable reason for rejection is fear of failure. Therefore, it may be just a matter of reducing the scope and resubmitting an addendum. In this scenario, investigate the possibility of building a smaller data mart versus a full-blown data warehouse. Reduce the users, number of tools, and amount of information to reduce the costs. Executives know that building a large data warehouse has a greater risk of failure than smaller data marts. Reducing the scope offers the business a proof of concept implementation option. The addendum would be a description of what has been reduced and the impact of the reduction. Remember to always agree with the executive management's decision to reject the original plan.

A lack of funds for information technology is becoming a more common reason for rejection. Funding may already be allocated to critical application needs. The most common scenario for a lack of funds today is the impact of funding for Year 2000 projects. Most information technology organizations waited too long to upgrade existing systems to support the new millennium. Therefore, information technology funding is allocated to upgrading all information systems. This scenario will be on every information technology top priority list until the year 2002.[8]

Fear not, when the desire and business needs are there for a data warehouse, there is opportunity to build one. The approach needs to be altered to work within these constraints. The information analysis phase is a common task across information technology systems. Therefore, review the scope of existing systems already approved. See if the scope of these approved projects can be expanded slightly to include any missing business subject areas (namely, any that are important to your needs). Identify if any of the work already accomplished by these projects can be reused and applied to the data warehouse. The objective is to identify an existing project whose scope, existing budget, and resources can be applied to your data warehouse project.

Although it would be easier to use projects within your business unit, it does not have to be limited to that area. Another business unit may be building a smaller data mart that satisfies most of the business's needs. Look to expand either the scope, the feeds, network access, or additional tools. This is the time to be resourceful until budget limitations subside. The data analyst or business information analyst will be able to assist in the investigation. Either individual has access to what other business units are planning and building.

Organizational control (politics) is a trickier issue and must be handled with care. Writing a business case, as described in this chapter, illustrates exactly what the business needs, its justification, and how it will be implemented. The style illustrates that the writer is well-organized and in control of the project and its risks. A great deal of investigative work has already been accomplished. Other business units smell success! Merely being a part of it is not enough for goal-seeking business managers. They want control, power, and success on their record. Therefore, do not be surprised if another business manager attempts to take over the project.[9] The business case may be rejected just so another business unit can apply for funding a remarkably similar project under their domain.

Be alert to this possibility. Anticipate this happening before you present the business case. Determine which alternative would be best for your business unit. It may not be worth the political fight to maintain control. If another group manages the project make sure that your business unit participates to ensure that your business unit's needs are satisfied. Alternatively, separate from that project completely. Reduce the original scope and build a smaller data mart as a separate project that is removed from other business managers.

If it still makes good business sense to maintain control and build the data warehouse as described in the business case, be prepared to be ahead of time. Keep your management line informed as to why it would be best for them, as well as for the corporation, for his or her unit to maintain control of the project. They will assist in maintaining control. They will play the political games for you.[10]

Summary

Implementing a data warehouse is a significant investment in time and money. However, the ROI can be realized by uncovering answers to difficult questions and being able to react to findings unknown before.

In order to obtain the proper funding and resources for any information technology project, you need the acceptance and support of executive management. This is obtained by writing and presenting a clear and concise business case. This chapter instructed the business executive or manager how to formulate and present a business case for a data warehouse project that will obtain the highest priority and funding from executive management.

A good business case will hold true throughout the life of the project. It will be reviewed at the end of each stage of development to compare the estimated and actual costs and benefits. Throughout the development of the data warehouse, the business case contributes to the justification for the continuance or termination of the project. By following the six steps outlined in this chapter, your chances for success are enhanced.

What to Do About Employee Training and Education

Technology professionals are not the only people in search of more information about data warehousing. Business professionals are searching for educational courses and case studies to assist them with their data warehouse projects. As data warehousing has grown in popularity, so has the material available to the business community.

This book is an excellent beginning for obtaining a ground-level understanding of data warehousing and what it can do for your corporation. Consider this book the first step — a springboard into the world of data warehousing. It provides an overview for people with minimal or no knowledge of the topic. This book introduces readers to basic concepts and assists them in determining the need for their corporations.

This chapter concentrates on the next step, if that need arises. Therefore, this chapter has two objectives: to explain where to find more information and to identify where to obtain assistance during any step of the implementation process.

To satisfy the first objective, this chapter provides additional sources of information about data warehousing in a training curriculum format. The training plan spans the life of the development of a data warehouse. Chapter 2, "How a Data Warehouse Is Built," describes how the evolutionary process of building a data warehouse is similar to any manufacturing process. This chapter will take a similar approach in correlating where and when to go for additional information about data warehousing.

The second objective of this chapter discusses where to go within the information technology organization for assistance. This includes the use of internal employees and external consultants within the information technology field. Topics include the type of individuals and their skill levels who are available for assistance at any step during the data warehouse process.

As with the rest of this book, this chapter is written for the business community. The recommendations in this chapter may contain technical information, but it is not overly complex. Therefore, the recommendations are valuable for the nontechnical business manager.

Additional information about data warehousing becomes available daily. All sources documented in this chapter provide avenues for investigating new and improved offerings in books, periodicals, and training. Some of the informational sources provided are web sites or periodicals that are consistently updated. Other additional sources for information are books that will be valid for years and overlap into other technological solutions.

Sources for Information

This section of the chapter provides sources of information for each step in the data warehouse process. As a reminder, the eight stages are summarized in Figure 7-1. The primary sources for information falls into the following categories:

- Books and periodicals

- Organizations

- Conferences

- Web pages

- Formal training (supplied by vendor and training companies)

Business users should not be reluctant to select any of these books or periodicals because of their titles. These sources are recommended with full knowledge of the business user's possible lack of technical background.

Step 1: The Idea

After reading this book, if you still require more information to help persuade your manager to research the data warehouse solution, the following sources may provide you additional information on the topic.

Figure 7-1. Training requirements throughout the data warehouse cycle.

Step	Description	Training Requirements	Primary Source
Step 1	The birth of an idea of a need and use for a data warehouse	Business uses for data warehouse	Business organizations
Step 2	Analyzing the feasibility and return on investment of building one	Success stories for data warehouse	Web, periodicals, conferences, IT organization
Step 3	Designing the data warehouse	Data warehouse requirements	Books, periodicals, IT organization, outside training organizations
Step 4	Developing the data warehouse	Data definition	Corporate dictionaries
Step 5	Assembling and testing the data warehouse	Using the data warehouse	Vendor of front-end tools
Step 6	Implementing the data warehouse	Using the data warehouse	Vendor of front-end tools
Step 7	Maintenance and enhancements to the data warehouse	Train new users	In-house training organizations
Step 8	Obsolescence of the data warehouse	None	Industry specialists

First, find out how other organizations have initiated a data warehouse project. Your best approach would be to call business organizations such as the American Management Association (www.amanet.org) or business organizations specific to your industry. They have access to business managers of all industries who can be contacted to discuss their successes or failures with data warehouses.

Next, read the nontechnical but technology-oriented periodicals, such as the ones written for chief information technology officers. *CIO Magazine* has been covering data warehousing since 1994. This monthly magazine keeps watch on the trends with respect to the uses and advantages of data warehouses. The magazine's web site (www.cio.org) provides links to articles and case studies plus a glossary of data warehousing terms.

There are organizations for industry analysts that contain several research articles about data warehouses. They provide general access from the web for older articles. However, your information technology organization must pay for access rights to more detailed information. If your information technology organization has a membership, you are able to "ask the experts" or read FAQs (frequently asked questions). Your question is submitted to a select group of experts who are knowledgeable about data warehousing. Examples of industry expert organizations are:

- Gartner Group: 408-486-7765; www.gartner.com

- GIGA Information Group:[1] www.gigaweb.com

- Meta Group: www.meta.com

Step 2: Analyze the Feasibility

The objective of step two is to build a business case for implementing a data warehouse. For this step, concentrate on identifying how your corporation will use one. Look for examples of how other organizations are using data warehousing and the type of tools most commonly used.

The first place to begin the investigation is at the Data Warehouse Institute (972-578-5022 or www.dw-institute.com). This organization is dedicated to developing the best practices for data warehousing professionals. They provide periodicals, books, conferences, and training for technicians as well as business professionals. The Data Warehouse Institute monitors the pulse of data warehousing, including the direction the technology is taking and successful implementation strategies. Their book *Data Mining: A Hands-On Approach for Business Professionals* provides information for the nontechnical professional about data mining and its recommended uses.

The Data Warehouse Institute provides several seminars throughout the country during each year. At their seminars, attendees have the opportunity to listen to visionaries, attend specific classes, view vendor products without pressure, and speak to other customers with similar business problems that data warehouses are solving. You can speak with experienced practitioners from both the technical and business sides of the organization. You can attend speeches given by the business community about their experiences, metrics used to determine success, and how the data warehouse is being used in their organizations.

The Data Warehouse Institute provides access to publications created by other organizations when the institute decides that such publications will be of significant help in implementing a data warehouse. One such book that will provide a great deal of value when developing the business case is *Data Warehousing: What Works?* This two-volume series contains case studies, articles, and a comprehensive directory of vendors.

Another popular source for information is the Data Communication Institute (DCI) (www.dci.com). DCI is an organization that provides training, consulting services, and seminars on a wide range of technological topics, one of which is data warehousing.

The Data Administration Management Association (DAMA) has both domestic and international chapters. They are an organization for data analysts (whose primary role is to build a business model that represents the data to be contained in the data warehouse). The association sponsors monthly meetings on topics that relate to data analysis. Both local and global web sites exist on both the world wide web and CompuServe. Within the web sites are forums or news groups available to ask questions about success strategies and opinions on specific data warehousing tools. You can access data analysts who have hands-on experience:

- In different industries

- With different data warehouse sizes

- Using different tools and platforms

William Inmon and Ralph Kimball have each written several books and articles about data warehousing. They are considered to be the fathers of data warehousing. However, most of the material is technical in nature. Their books may be useful for identifying the costs of implementing a data warehouse. Some of their books include:

- *Building the Data Warehouse,* 2nd edition (New York: John Wiley & Sons, 1996)

- *Managing the Data Warehouse* (New York: John Wiley & Sons, 1997)

- *Practical Techniques for Building Dimensional Data Warehouses* (New York: John Wiley & Sons, 1996)

- *Using the Data Warehouse* (New York: John Wiley & Sons, 1994)

There is a process for developing and implementing a data warehouse. The tasks, roles, responsibilities, milestones, and deliverables are all part of this process. Platinum Technology/LBMS[2] (www.platinum.com) has a product that contains template development plans for building data warehouses, including how to select user tools. Their templates are based upon the best practices for implementing a data warehouse and contain all the parts of a good process along with checklists, glossary, and metric formulas to assist in planning the project. If your information technology organization has purchased this process management tool, you may wish to read its contents to help you develop the implementation plan section of your business case.

Books are available that define the data warehouse implementation process, such as:

- Anahory, Sam & Dennis Murray, *Data Warehousing in the Real World.* Reading, Mass.: Addison-Wesley.

- *Planning a Data Warehouse Project* by Michael Haisten of Vital Technologies.

- Simon, Alan R., *Data Warehousing for Dummies.* San Mateo, Calif.: IDG Books Worldwide.

Step 3: Designing the Data Warehouse

At this point, it might prove beneficial to understand the requirements for designing a data warehouse, including how to gather and document requirements and build a business model that depicts your data needs and usage. It is important to realize that every data warehouse project is unique. The opportunities and challenges will differ for every organization. However, some key issues are similar for every organization. For gathering, documenting, and confirming business requirements, the following books are recommended for the businessperson to investigate.

These books will assist in developing the requirements and working with the information technology community. These particular books are not so deep into the process that they will allow the business user to develop a data warehouse without the assistance of information technologists. However, they will educate the reader on defining and documenting the contents and use of the data warehouse.

- Bruce, Thomas A., *Designing Quality Databases With IDEF1X Information Models.* New York: Dorset House Publishing, 1992.[3]

- Flavin, Matt. *Fundamental Concepts of Information Modeling.* Englewood Cliffs, N.J.: Yourdon Press, 1981.

- Gause, Donald C., and Gerald Weinberg. *Are Your Lights On? How to Know What the Problem Really Is*, 2nd ed. New York: Dorset House Publishing, 1990.

- ———. *Exploring Requirements: Quality Before Design.* New York: Dorset House Publishing, 1989.

- Robertson, Susan and James. *Complete Systems Analysis.* New York: Dorset House, 1996.

If your data warehouse project involves several individuals from the business community to develop the requirements, you may wish to investigate bringing a requirement class in-house. Training organizations that have specific data warehouse courses are typically geared toward technicians. Other training organizations that have courses geared toward the business community do not have courses specifically for data warehousing. Vendors may but they will obviously be gearing their training courses and seminars toward their own products. A small sampling of sources for nonvendor training during the requirement gathering phases are as follows:

- Data Warehouse Institute, 972-578-5022 (www.ebgconsulting.com). Provides courses on the basic concepts of data warehousing.

- EGB Consulting, 317-844-3747. Provides courses on modeling techniques for the business community.

- Marie Buretta, Inc., 609-987-1770 (www.mburetta.com) Provides modeling and data warehouse training.

- Knowledge Partners, Inc., 973-543-9820 (www.kplusa.com) Provides courses on modeling techniques for the business community.

- Saddle Island Institute, 617-720-9545. Provides courses and one-day seminars on data warehousing.

- Spectrum Technologies Group, 908-725-4000. Provides courses on modeling techniques for the business community, as well as data warehousing consulting services.

- Strategic Business Decisions, Inc., 973-509-9427, sbdipat@home.com. Provides courses for the business community on the software

development process and how to identify and document requirements. Provides consultants to assist the business community in
preparing and developing a data warehouse.

- Strategic Business Solutions, Inc., a consulting company specializing in the design, development, and implementation of the data
  warehouse. Specifically, Vidette Poe, author of *Building a Data
  Warehouse for Decision Support*, provides onsite training courses
  on building a data warehouse (WAREHS@aol.com).

- Tryon & Associates, 918-455-3300, catryon@aol.com. Courses for
  the business community and the information technology organization on the software development analysis process.

- Weinberg & Weinberg, www.geraldmweinberg.com. Offers an excellent series of courses and consulting services on problem solving
  and the human aspects of implementing technological solutions.

Do not limit yourself to specialized training organizations. Many uni-
versities have departments dedicated to data warehousing, for example:

- University of Binghamton

- University of Colorado

- University of Georgia

- University of Hawaii

- University of Manitoba

Step 4: Developing the Data Warehouse

At this point, you want to begin to develop in-house training for the business community. You have already identified what data to capture and the
source for all the information. Most of the data should be defined and its
definition agreed to during this step. As a result, a corporate dictionary of
terms is developed. For this, it is recommended to use industry specific
dictionaries (finance, insurance, or medical) as the base for all terminology. This will prevent any misinterpretations between business units.

It is also the time to prepare yourself to use the data warehouse. Select
books on statistical analysis for your area of expertise, for example, books
on forecasting or market trend analysis. These types of books will assist in

developing the requirements for the data warehouse. They will also provide ideas about what type of tools you will require when accessing information from an implemented data warehouse.

The demand for data warehousing is growing. The rapid evolution of data warehousing tools makes it difficult to determine which products are appropriate for supporting your data warehousing requirements. It is important to read the vendor material carefully against your list of tool requirements. The specialized tools supplied by vendors that require training fall into one of the following categories:

- Data warehousing

- Data mining

- Visualization tools

- Information access providers

- Query managers and report writers

- Spreadsheets

- Multidimensional databases

- Statistical analysis

- Artificial intelligence and advanced analysis tools

- Graphical display

Again, the Data Warehouse Institute provides books on selecting the right tools for the data warehouse. Two such books are:

- *Choosing the Right Tools: An Unbiased Assessment of Databases, Data Transformation, and End-User Access Tools*

- *How to Determine the Best Tools to Deliver Warehouse Information to the Desktop*

Steps 5 and 6: Assembling, Testing, and Implementing the Data Warehouse

While the data warehouse is being assembled, concentrate on vendor-product training. Training web sites exist that link to vendor-supplied training (such as www.trregistry.com). Begin to identify what training your users will require.[4] Research training for the specific products that you plan to purchase. Use this time to develop an introduction to data warehousing for the business community. Follow up with courses on the specific tools that will be purchased by the business community.

Include in the training curriculum a general course on data warehousing. The Data Warehouse Institute provides courses for purchase. A sample from their data warehousing curriculum includes:

- Data Warehousing 101: A Practical Overview

- Data Warehouse Step by Step by The Vital Connection

- A Seminar in Data Mining and Knowledge Discovery

Step 7: Maintaining the Data Warehouse

During the previous steps of the data warehouse process, measures should have been taken to develop in-house training. The data warehouse training curriculum should be reviewed on a consistent basis. New tools should be investigated to see if they could provide the business community with better access to the data warehouse and use it more effectively. As a result, the training curriculum should be reviewed on a regular basis (quarterly or twice a year minimally) and adjusted to reflect new and improved tools. The courses should be reevaluated with every incremental release to determine if all the new users' needs will be met by the current curriculum. Improvements to the current curriculum should be incorporated to improve the business community's use of the data warehouse. Forgetting to review and improve the data warehouse's curriculum will bring the end of its usefulness to the corporation at a faster rate.

Step 8: Obsolescence

A time will come when the data warehouse will cost more to maintain than the value achieved from the data contained within it. At this point, the sources mentioned throughout this chapter are not obsolete. Instead, the sources should be continually reviewed for the next evolution of the data warehouse. The World Wide Web should be the main source for identifying future trends. Use the Internet to follow trends in your industry as well as technological evolution. This chapter mentioned many URLs[5] for popular data warehouse information that also support evolutionary trends. Do not worry, data warehousing is still in its infancy. However, mark these URLs in your Internet bookmarks to become a knowledge expert for your business organization. After all, since you were the driving force for implementing a successful data warehouse, why shouldn't you be chosen for the next project that integrates business and technology?

Sources for Assistance

The previous section discussed the types of training and sample sources for each step in the data warehousing process. There is another source for more information that is applicable for all steps, which includes:

- Individuals who are in-house (employees)
- Individuals who are hired by the information technology organization (individual consultants or consulting companies)
- Individuals who are hired by the business organization (individual consultants or consulting companies)
- Vendors who are hired by the information technology organization or by the business organization
- In-house training

The following section provides an overview of these additional sources for questions, recommendations, and assistance.

In-House Technicians

Do not discount people within your information technology organization. Many individuals with experience in data can help answer your questions. Depending upon the size of your corporation, you may have individuals within a specialized data warehouse department ranging from seven to twenty-five professionals. If a data warehousing or another type of decision support or customer information department does not exists in your organization, a group specializing in data analysis or just analysis may be the point of contact. If neither of the above scenarios exist, the project leader of software or application development for your area will be first point of contact.

The first scenario described in the previous paragraph represents organizations that currently have some sort of data warehouse implemented. The organization structure could be of two types. Each type depends upon the size and maturity of the data warehouse implementation. Figure 7-2 illustrates the organizational structure for a small corporation that has already implemented a data warehouse. These are roles and responsibilities of between one to four individuals. In this type of organizational structure, you have a manager of the project, a programmer/analyst, an architect, and a systems programmer. The manager should be your first point of contact when questions arise. It is his or her responsibility to assign and introduce you to a programmer analyst. The decision support programmer/analyst will act as the user liaison. This individual understands on-line analytical processing and can provide insight into how the business requirements can be satisfied by a data warehouse. The architect will design the data warehouse. The systems programmer(s) will implement the physical data warehouse.

Figure 7-3 illustrates an organization that has installed a large data warehouse. It was probably determined that the data warehouse is a mission-critical application for the business community. The organization has determined that the data warehouse warrants specialty roles to develop and support this application. Again, in this type of organization, your first point of contact for any type of question should be either the front-end manager or the director. During the development of the business requirements, your primary contact is the decision support system (DSS) analyst or programmer. Business requirements, in this scenario, include the selection and purchase of user-friendly front-end tools for the business community's use.

The second scenario is probably the most common information technology organizational structure found in Fortune 500 companies. Figure 7-4 provides a full picture of how the data organization fits into the entire information technology organization. In this scenario, the organization has a support group dedicated to analysis (data or process). This support group could be part of a support organization or contained within the business application area.

Four roles that will assist and interface with the business community on a frequent basis include:

- Data analyst/architect

- Business analyst

Figure 7-2. Small organization data warehouse team structure.

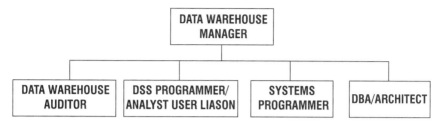

The Data Warehousing Institute, *The 1996 Summary of Roles & Responsiblities of Data Warehousing Professionals*, p. 2. Reprinted by permission of The Data Warehousing Institute, Gaithersburg, Maryland (www.dw-institute.com).

Figure 7-3. Large organization data warehouse team structure.

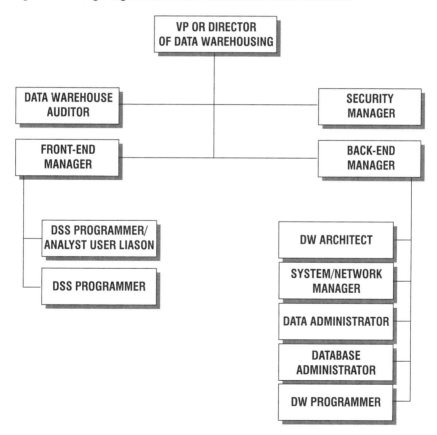

The Data Warehousing Institute, *The 1996 Summary of Roles & Responsiblities of Data Warehousing Professionals*, p. 3. Reprinted by permission of The Data Warehousing Institute, Gaithersburg, Maryland (www.dw-institute.com).

Figure 7-4. View of a typical information technology organization.

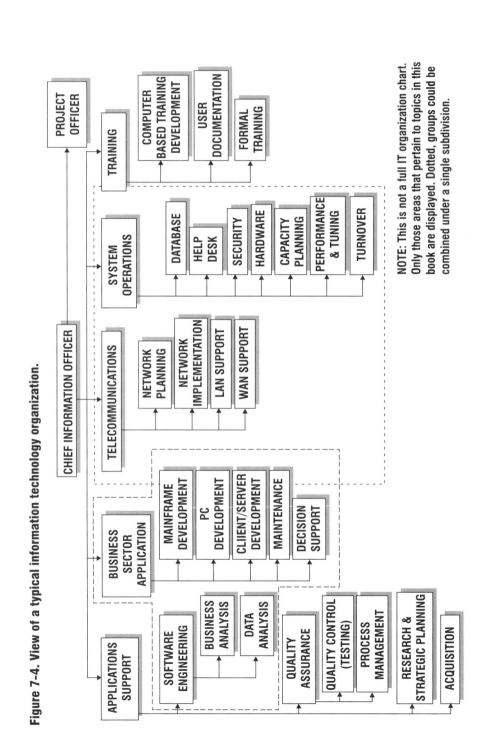

NOTE: This is not a full IT organization chart. Only those areas that pertain to topics in this book are displayed. Dotted, groups could be combined under a single subdivision.

- Requirements engineer[6]

- Project leader/manager

The data analysts are responsible for analyzing the business's information or data requirements. They build models of information to represent the business. They keep the whole organization's needs in mind instead of each individual department's view. It is this group's role to build the infrastructure for business information in a concise and usable manner. Their focus is not on individual requirements but on the entire company's information infrastructure. Data analysts are trained to assist the business representative in broadening his or her ideas and to identify and expand on information requirements that enhance business. Data analysts will ask the business representative questions about what information is needed and how it is to be used.

The business analysts specialize in work flow or process analysis. They analyze the business process flow to determine the ultimate use of processes to fulfill business requirements. They uncover the business events and process restrictions[7] that the data warehouse must support. On many projects, the person assigned as the business analyst will also take on the role of spokesperson for the business representative. As a result, they usually remain with the project from inception to implementation, ensuring that the business representative's needs and requirements are met. As stated previously, it is important to remember that business analysts are good people with whom to stay in contact. They are a source of information on who, how, and why something is needed during the development process. They can also keep you posted on project status and when and how to intercept any smoke screens.

The requirements engineer is a new role that is currently evolving in the information technology organization. This person differs from the data analyst and business analyst since he or she is responsible for all requirements. Generally speaking, requirements may not always evolve into a data warehouse or other information technology solution. The requirements may impact a business product, service or organization. The responsibility of the requirements engineer is to elicit, analyze, document, validate, and manage all levels of requirements throughout the development, implementation, and continual maintenance of each requirement. For a data warehouse project, the role of requirements engineer may be synonymous with data analyst and business analyst. The other possibility is that the requirements engineer is the first person who elicits the initial high-level requirements and transfers the detailed analysis to one of the other roles. In either situation, the requirements engineer will be responsible for ensuring that the requirements are maintained as they change and are implemented as required.

The success of any project is never due to one exceptional person. A successful project occurs through the efforts of many people and extends beyond department boundaries. These people make up the project's team. Teams consist of many individuals who have varying levels of skills, talents, work styles, and knowledge. The project leader is responsible for coordinating the development efforts of the team within the constraints of the information technology organization. The role of project leader is one of the most complex within the information technology organization. The project leader is responsible for motivating the team to achieve the business objectives in a productive and economical manner. This position requires the use of both technical and people skills. The business representative who is responsible for day-to-day contact with the information technology organization should meet with the project leader throughout the development process on a regular basis.

Independent Consultant Considerations

If the project requires the hiring of independent consultants, most will be hired by the information technology organization to represent their interests. However, the business community may wish to hire a consultant to assist with:

- Scoping
- Requirements gathering
- Business case development
- Analysis
- Implementation
- Training

With hundreds of choices of data warehouse experts, it is difficult to know which companies or individuals really possess the expertise that your corporation needs. Understanding your team's strengths and identifying knowledge gaps begins the process of selecting the right consultant for your specific environment. The truth is that one size does not fit all organizations.

Consulting expertise differs greatly. Vendor-product consultants may lead to biased requirements that favor the strengths of a particular product and then push for their product's implementation.

Whether business knowledge carries equal weight to technology and product knowledge is a constant debate. It depends upon the needs that the individual consultant will satisfy and your comfort level. Having business knowledge may quicken the analysis effort. The individual will not require detailed explanations of key business terms. Your valuable time may be minimized when you hire a consultant to speak for you.

The double-edged sword is that the individual may have a different or preconceived opinion of how the data should be organized and used. The individual may implement what he or she learned from previous clients in the same industry. To minimize this risk, make certain that the business consultant understands your interpretation of the data and the value it may provide and that the individual can and will listen.[8]

An alternative to hiring a consultant who understands the business more than data warehousing development is to hire an individual who is either a data analyst or business information analyst. They are trained to listen and understand the capabilities of a data warehouse. However, it is important to have an information technician from your organization involved in the interviewing process.

Corporations successfully utilize outside consultants on data warehouse projects by understanding the different types of specialists and integrating their knowledge. Understand what you should expect to pay for those individuals. Interface with consultants as you do with employees. Treat them with respect and not as an interchangeable piece of property. The road to building and implementing a data warehouse is long. Resource turnover is inevitable but should be kept to a minimum to avoid any additional delays in the implementation.

The price for data warehouse expertise varies by skill level, and geographical supply and demand. Individual data warehouse consultants prefer an hourly rate. Professional days (eight to ten hours) may be negotiated. However, top data warehouse consultants usually quote a ten to twelve hour-day rate to compensate for the professional day. Therefore, do not shy away from hourly rate consultants. You may actually be getting more for your money.

Many organizations exist that have employees who specialize in data warehousing. Examples are the larger accounting firms that also have a technology division. In this situation, the division would have one or more individuals who specialize in data warehousing. These individuals can be brought in either through the business or technology division of your corporation. They are available for consultation at any step of the data warehousing process. However, these companies command top dollar for a professional day's work. Some of the larger consulting organizations, other than the large-size accounting firms, are:

- American Management Systems: 703-227-6066 (www.amsinc.com)

- Cap Gemini: (www.capgemini.com)

- Data Warehousing Institute: 972-578-5022 (www.dw-institute.com)

- IBM: (www.ibm.com)

- EBG Consulting: 317-844-3747 (www.ebgconsulting.com)

- Marie Buretta, Inc.: 609-987-1770 (www.mburetta.com)

- Knowledge Partners, Inc.: 973-543-9820 (www.kpiusa.com)

- Patricia Seybold Group: 617-742-5200 (www.psgroup.com)

- Strategic Business Decisions, Inc.: 973-509-9427

- VITAL Connection: 408-723-3270

Product Vendors

Product suppliers for data warehouse-related hardware and software are growing daily. Therefore, search the Internet for data waehousing to identify the list. Any vendor will have a dog-and-pony show that will discuss what a data warehouse is along with what their product will do for you. The business community should have the final say on any front-end software product that they will use to interface with the data warehouse. However, if the business community decides to initiate contact with any vendor and requests a demonstration of their product, include someone from the information technology organization. They will ensure that the product works with the other pieces of the data warehouse solution. Although this is by no means a comprehensive list, some key players in the data warehousing arena include:

- Acta Technology
- Brio Technology
- Business Objects
- Cognos
- IBM
- Information Builders
- MicroStrategy
- NCR
- Oracle Corporation
- Planning Sciences
- Platinum Technology
- Seagate Software

Training

Training materials are one of the most important and quickly forgotten items that need to be included early in the development of the business requirements. When people remember to develop training materials, the effort involved in them is underestimated. It takes a great deal of time to develop good quality training materials, which require a great deal of the business representative's time. The creators of the training materials need to understand the needs of the eventual users of the system as well as how the system works. However, good documentation prepared during the analysis and design of the system will lessen the amount of time required from the business representative.

A training department is responsible for all training-related activities. The department develops computer based training (CBT) development, user documentation, and formal training. The department usually involves more than one technical writer who also possesses personal computer knowledge. A growing trend, due to the influx of Internet users, is to outsource the writing effort to professional technical writer consultants. The system and documentation could be sent through the Internet with follow-up questions handled either by short telephone calls or through Internet messages.

Summary

Almost without exception, data warehousing is a costly and time-consuming venture. However, the competitive advantage that superior business intelligence from a data warehouse provides may be priceless. Embarking on a data warehouse journey without proper training is one of the sticks that could break the camel's back. This book covers the basics. However, additional training may be required throughout the actual data warehouse implementation process. This chapter introduced a training curriculum and sources for more information about data warehousing. Use this chapter throughout the design, development, and implementation of the data warehouse as a source for additional information.

8

Parting Thoughts

The business community is learning about the possibilities of data warehousing from reading business publications, attending conferences, their competitors and clients, and, of course, their information technology organization. They are learning that data warehouses can provide business personnel with a new medium for accessing data that will enable their organization to grow into the future. They are learning that data warehouses have now become mission-critical applications for survival in the competitive global marketplace. However, the business community does not understand how or why.

Data Warehousing Advice for Managers has been written for the business community. By explaining the topic in business language, the business manager can understand why his or her corporation must act to implement a data warehouse. The idea for this book came about because of the growing interest in and popularity of data warehousing. However, it has been the experience of the author that many data warehousing projects fail. The main reason is because information technicians are running the data warehouse project instead of the business community. Business personnel understand business. They understand the need and use of the data that will be contained in the data warehouse. Information technicians understand technology. They see it as a new toy that will enhance their marketability. In order for a data warehouse to be successful, an understanding of both business and technology is needed for this costly project to succeed. However, the driving force behind implementing a data warehouse must be from the business community.

To facilitate the merging of business and technology into a successfully implemented data warehouse, this book was written to put the control of the effort in the hands of the business community. This book introduces the business manager to a technology that will dramatically enhance the corporation's ability to be competitive. The book covers the following important topics:

Chapter 1, "Data Warehousing," introduces the business manager to the topic of data warehousing. It provides a framework for the business manager to understand the many facets of the subject, including an understanding of what a data warehouse is, what can it do for the company, and a review of how competitors are using the product.

Chapter 2, "How a Data Warehouse Is Built," describes the efforts involved in implementing a data warehouse. This chapter provides the business managers with an understanding of the level of their involvement and exposure as to why the development costs are so high. This chapter provides enough information for the business manager to "manage" the implementation effort.

Chapter 3, "Keys to a Successful Implementation," provides the business manager with insight into keys for a successful implementation and common reasons for failure. With this knowledge, the business manager will be able to control the effort of implementing a data warehouse to ensure a positive ROI for the corporation and to ensure that the needs of the business are met.

Chapter 4, "What Do I Do With It Now?" discusses what to do with the data warehouse once the business community has access to the data. This encompasses two focuses. The first is to describe the business manager's role and responsibilities after the implementation of the data warehouse, which includes a discussion of topics that will ensure the continues success of the data warehouse until its obsolescence. The second part of this chapter illustrated that the data warehouse's power intensifies when it is combined with other technology. Other technologies can be implemented with the initial implementation or can be added as the experience of the business community increases. The point is that a data warehouse is a pool of data. Other technology, such as data mining and the Internet, provides the usability and access to the data pool.

Chapter 5: "How to Write a Winning Business Case." After reading the previous four chapters, the business manager has probably identified the need and wants to proceed with implementing a data warehouse in his or her organization. "How to Write a Winning Business Case" assists the business manager in initiating the data warehouse project. Even if standards are available within the organization, this chapter discussed specifics that are important in developing a business case for a data warehouse project.

Chapter 6, "Selling the Winning Business Case." Writing a winning business case is only part of the battle to obtain sufficient funding. The best-written business case can be lost on the executive committee's desk. To ensure that your proposal does not end up lost, a presentation must be organized, scheduled, and presented to the key decision makers. "Selling the Winning Business Case" takes the reader through the steps of presenting the business case in a manner that will summarize key points to the decision makers. This will enable the executive committee to quickly and clearly identify the need for a data warehouse project. The outcome of the presentation will be sufficient staffing and funding for this mission-critical project.

Chapter 7, "What to Do About Employee Training and Education," discusses where more information can be obtained by the business community about data warehouses. The information in this chapter will assist the business manager throughout the life of the data warehouse. Therefore, this book is an excellent reference to be used throughout the life of the data warehouse to keep current about:

- Competitive uses for data warehouses (case studies)

- Training courses and books for new users

- Technological advances that will improve a company's data warehouse

Next Steps

This book makes the business manager comfortable with the subject of data warehousing and its related technology. With knowledge obtained from this book, the business manager is able to determine whether or not a data warehouse will provide the competitive advantage that the corporation requires in the next millennium. Therefore, it is important for the business manager to begin thinking about how to implement the data warehouse at his or her organization. To kick off the effort, the following list of ten to-do items, all of which were discussed in detail in this book, should be added to the business manager's task list.

1. Identify the business problem or opportunity the data warehouse will satisfy.

2. Itemize how a data warehouse can be used by the organization.

3. Document how the current situation cannot satisfy business needs.

4. Document the business areas or subjects that the data warehouse will support.

5. Itemize specific data requirements for these business areas.

6. Itemize when the most current information needs to be available to the user community.

7. Determine the location of the business users of the data warehouse.

8. Determine the analytical requirements.

9. Identify measures for the data warehouse's success.

10. Arrange a meeting with the data warehousing expert in the information technology organization (or hire an expert consultant).

Summary

This book provides the business manager with information that will enhance the corporation's competitive advantage. What is now important is to act on what was read. Begin by scheduling the ten immediate to-do items. Take advantage of the information technology organization being busy working on the Year 2000 issue. Be prepared for when they are available to implement your data warehouse by having the requirements, and possibly even the design, complete. Chances are, your competition has already started down this path. Wait and the competition will surpass you. Begin learning and preparing for what has to be done to implement your company's mission-critical data warehouse. Use your time wisely:

- By increasing your knowledge about data warehousing

- By thinking of requirements for the data warehouse

- By thinking about infrastructure issues and what other technology will enhance the data warehouse's success

- By developing the winning business case for a data warehouse

Sample Data Warehouse Work Breakdown Structure Template

This appendix contains a sample data warehouse project work breakdown template. Many exist in the industry that can be purchased from consulting companies and software vendors.[1] They vary in terminology and approaches. This particular template[2] uses the incremental framework described in Chapter 2, "How a Data Warehouse Is Built." The template does not imply a waterfall or linear approach. At a minimum, steps 4 through 7 would be followed for each incremental release of a data warehouse's new functionality.

This template is for reference only. It does not contain a comprehensive list of tasks for designing, building, and implementing a data warehouse. The tasks listed in the template can be broken down further into specific subtasks. This template is provided to further illustrate the complexity of the process. The information technology organization within your corporation will develop a template and schedule based upon corporate standards, experience, project characteristics, scope, and available resources. The business manager should insist on being involved in the development and review of the plan. Before each step is finished, a checkpoint should take place. At each checkpoint, all deliverable work products should be reviewed by the business manager and knowledge expert. At each checkpoint, the next step should be reviewed and the schedule adjusted with new information. The next step should not occur without the business manager's approval and appropriate funding and resource allocation.

Step 1: Birth of an Idea

Activity 1.1: *Current Situation*

Task 1.1.1: Investigate data currently used by business

Task 1.1.2: Investigate how data is used and manipulated

Task 1.1.3: Investigate current data impact on business work flow (caused by which business events and timings)

Task 1.1.4: Document current situation

Task 1.1.5: Document business impact of current situation

Activity 1.2: *Define Possibilities*

Task 1.2.1: Identify requirements for new or improved data

Task 1.2.2: Identify requirements to improve data work flow

Task 1.2.3: Identify requirements for data usage

Task 1.2.4: Outline potential improvements to current situation

Task 1.2.5: Document potential business opportunity

Activity 1.3: *Define Plan of Action*

Task 1.3.1: Research data warehouse opportunities

Task 1.3.2: Document impact of not implementing a data warehouse

Task 1.3.3: Document possible tangible and intangible benefits with a data warehouse solution

Task 1.3.4: Develop plan for developing a formal business case

Activity 1.4: *Present Business Idea*

Task 1.4.1: Document business idea

Task 1.4.2: Present to management

Task 1.4.3: Obtain approval to develop business case

Step 2: Analyzing the Feasibility

Activity 2.1: *Refine Scope*

Task 2.1.1:   Contact information technologists for assistance

Task 2.1.2:   Identify key stakeholders for data warehouse

Task 2.1.3:   Identify subject matter experts

Task 2.1.4:   Identify key business areas

Task 2.1.5:   Identify data requirements by each business area

Task 2.1.6:   Identify key business measures

Task 2.1.7:   Identify business events and timings

Task 2.1.8:   Identify query usage

Task 2.1.9:   Identify user locations

Task 2.1.10: Document data requirements by user and location

Task 2.1.11: Document response time requirements

Task 2.1.12: Document user access requirements

Task 2.1.13: Prioritize requirements

Task 2.1.14: Document requirements model

Activity 2.2:   *Business Systems Options*

Task 2.2.1:   Consider buy/build and combination options

Task 2.2.2:   Determine user needs for data warehouse access

Task 2.2.3:   Determine required tools to support effort

Task 2.2.4:   Define alternative solutions

Task 2.2.5:   Evaluate alternative solutions

Task 2.2.6:   Develop tool selection criteria

Task 2.2.7:   Develop RFI/RFP[3] for vendors

Task 2.2.8:   Review RFI/RFP

Task 2.2.9:   Select best-fit vendors for each tool type

Activity 2.3: *Proposed Costs*

Task 2.3.1:   Identify software requirements

Task 2.3.2:   Identify hardware requirements

Task 2.3.3:   Identify development costs

Task 2.3.4:   Identify training costs

Activity 2.4:   *Write Business Case[4]*

Task 2.4.1:   Document data warehouse strategy

Task 2.4.2:   Document plan to implement

Task 2.4.3:   Document tangible and intangible benefits

Task 2.4.4:   Document costs

Task 2.4.5:   Document recommendation

Task 2.4.6:   Assemble business case

Task 2.4.7:   Distribute to key stakeholders and decision makers

Activity 2.5:   *Present Business Case[5]*

Task 2.5.1:   Schedule presentation

Task 2.5.2:   Develop presentation material from the business case

Task 2.5.3:   Present to decision makers

Task 2.5.4:   Obtain executive approval to continue through next step

Step 3: Designing the Data Warehouse

Activity 3.1:   *Architecture Definition*

Task 3.1.1:   Establish security requirements

Task 3.1.2:   Define detailed business rules and logic

Task 3.1.3:   Identify data sources

Task 3.1.4:   Select architecture solution

Task 3.1.5:   Set up development environment

Task 3.1.6:   Set up test environment

Task 3.1.7:   Order required software

Task 3.1.8:   Order required hardware

Activity 3.2: *Data Warehouse Design*

Task 3.2.1: Create dimensional model

Task 3.2.2: Size data warehouse

Task 3.2.3: Identify keys and attributes

Task 3.2.4: Define system of record

Task 3.2.5: Define metadata

Task 3.2.6: Develop extract and load strategy

Task 3.2.7: Develop data distribution strategy

Task 3.2.8: Determine replication needs

Activity 3.3: *Delivery Planning*

Task 3.3.1: Define delivery increments

Task 3.3.2: Plan delivery increments

Task 3.3.3: Define increment acceptance criteria

Task 3.3.4: Establish program management procedures

Task 3.3.5: Define audit and control requirements

Task 3.3.6: Define data retention requirements

Task 3.3.7: Specify fallback and data recovery procedures

Task 3.3.8: Evaluate storage requirements

Task 3.3.9: Create performance predictions

Activity 3.4: *Extract and Load Planning*

Task 3.4.1: Define means to extract system of record

Task 3.4.2: Specify data transformation rules

Task 3.4.3: Specify data distribution and replication locations

Activity 3.5: *Technical Configuration Definition*

Task 3.5.1: Establish base technical configuration

Task 3.5.2: Establish development and delivery environment

Task 3.5.3:   Establish configuration management procedures

Task 3.5.4:   Establish response time requirements

Step 4: Developing the Data Warehouse

Activity 4.1: Develop code

Task 4.1.1:   Generate data transformation code

Task 4.1.2:   Generate code to produce standard reports

Task 4.1.3:   Generate code for standard inquiries

Task 4.1.4:   Generate code for data distribution and replication

Task 4.1.5:   Unit test code

Activity 4.2: Define Test Strategy

Task 4.2.1:   Define test strategy

Task 4.2.2:   Develop test plan

Task 4.2.3:   Create test scripts (hardware and software)

Task 4.2.4:   Create test cases

Task 4.2.5:   Define test package

Task 4.2.6:   Document acceptance criteria

Activity 4.3: Technical Architecture Pilot

Task 4.3.1:   Install and configure architecture

Task 4.3.2:   Develop pilot to test architecture

Task 4.3.3:   Evaluate architecture pilot

Task 4.3.4:   Revise technical architecture

Task 4.3.5:   Review results of technical architecture pilot

Activity 4.4: User Education

Task 4.4.1:   Identify training requirements

Task 4.4.2:   Develop training plan

Task 4.4.3:   Develop user training materials

Task 4.4.4: Create data warehouse operations guide

Task 4.4.5: Create data warehouse user guide

Task 4.4.6: Develop or customize training material

Task 4.4.7: Schedule tool training

Task 4.4.8: Schedule data warehouse business training

Task 4.4.9: Conduct training

Task 4.4.10: Review results of training

Step 5: Assembling and Testing the Data Warehouse

Activity 5.1: Extract and Load Development

Task 5.1.1: Test extraction and load utilities

Task 5.1.2: Populate data warehouse database

Task 5.1.3: Distribute and replicate database

Activity 5.2: Testing

Task 5.2.1: Establish test environment

Task 5.2.2: Perform test

Task 5.2.3: Log results

Task 5.2.4: Review test coverage

Task 5.2.5: Document defects

Task 5.2.6: Plan correction implementation

Activity 5.3: Data Access Development

Task 5.3.1: Design data access

Task 5.3.2: Design reports and queries

Task 5.3.3: Validate queries with users

Task 5.3.4: Define required changes

Activity 5.4: Target Environment

Task 5.4.1: Design workstation and network configuration

Task 5.4.2:   Design data warehouse security

Task 5.4.3:   Design warehouse subscription and authorization

Task 5.4.4:   System management strategy

Step 6: Implementing a Data Warehouse

Activity 6.1:   User Training

Task 6.1.1:   Pilot user-training and procedures

Task 6.1.2:   Evaluate course effectiveness

Task 6.1.3:   Update course material

Task 6.1.4:   Schedule formal training

Activity 6.2:   Data Warehouse Population

Task 6.2.1:   Initiate extract and load

Task 6.2.2:   Install network hardware and software

Task 6.2.3:   Distribute and replicate data onto appropriate servers

Task 6.2.4:   Install user-access tools

Task 6.2.5:   Enable user access

Activity 6.3:   Acceptance Testing

Task 6.3.1:   Create acceptance test scripts

Task 6.3.2:   Validate data distribution and replication

Task 6.3.3:   Validate security access

Task 6.3.4:   Review performance logs

Task 6.3.5:   Perform acceptance tests

Task 6.3.6:   Review results of acceptance testing

Activity 6.4:   Turnover

Task 6.4.1:   Install access system

Task 6.4.2:   Initiate production loads

Task 6.4.3:   Conduct user training

Task 6.4.4:   Evaluate user procedures and training

Task 6.4.5:   Initiate monitoring procedures

Step 7: Maintaining and Enhancing the Data Warehouse

Activity 7.1:   Performance

Task 7.1.1:   Monitor usage

Task 7.1.2:   Document measurement statistical results

Task 7.1.3:   Evaluate performance statistics

Task 7.1.4:   Document inconsistencies

Task 7.1.5:   Determine causes

Task 7.1.6:   Evaluate options

Task 7.1.7:   Document required enhancements

Task 7.1.8:   Optimize performance

Activity 7.2:   Training

Task 7.2.1:   Review results of usage

Task 7.2.2:   Identify gaps in training

Task 7.2.3:   Update training plan

Task 7.2.4:   Schedule training

Activity 7.3:   Defect Tracking and Resolution

Task 7.3.1:   Review data quality

Task 7.3.2:   Review issue log

Task 7.3.3:   Categorize defects

Task 7.3.4:   Analyze defect trends

Task 7.3.5:   Determine cause

Task 7.3.6:   Analyze impact

Task 7.3.7:   Document resolution

Task 7.3.8:   Prioritize defects and resolution

Task 7.3.9:   Plan correction implementation

Activity 7.4: Enhancement

Task 7.4.1:   Review query usage

Task 7.4.2:   Review data coverage

Task 7.4.3:   Review business coverage

Task 7.4.4:   Review enhancement requests

Task 7.4.5:   Analyze impact on data warehouse infrastructure

Task 7.4.6:   Analyze impact on data warehouse architecture

Task 7.4.7:   Prioritize enhancements for next incremental release

Step 8: Obsolescence

Activity 8.1:   Current Effectiveness

Task 8.1.1:   Gather statistics on current usage

Task 8.1.2:   Determine data quality

Task 8.1.3:   Determine query usage

Task 8.1.4:   Gather maintenance costs

Task 8.1.5:   Document user perception of effectiveness

Task 8.1.6:   Determine current return on investment

Task 8.1.7:   Document current situation with data warehouse

Activity 8.2:   Success Characteristics

Task 8.2.1:   Document growth trends from first incremental release
               to last

Task 8.2.2:   Identify reason for change in trend

Task 8.2.3:   Determine areas for opportunity

Activity 8.3:   Recommendation

Task 8.3.1:   Document current situation

Task 8.3.2:   Compare statistics to original business case

Task 8.3.3: Identify options

Task 8.3.4: Research options

Task 8.3.5: Select best options

Task 8.3.6: Determine migration issues

Task 8.3.7: Determine how current user needs will continue to be met

Task 8.3.8: Document recommendation

Technophobia Avoidance Glossary

The glossary contains terms that the business manager may come across in reading or when talking with information technologists. Some of these terms have been used throughout this book. These buzz words can confuse anyone new to the data warehouse environment. The definitions use nonprofessional terminology to give the reader confidence when discussing data warehousing. Therefore, this glossary alleviates any anxiety a business manager may feel about working with data warehouse technology by simplifying the terms for easier comprehension. This glossary will prove valuable throughout the steps of conceiving the idea to maintaining an implemented data warehouse.

This glossary contains abbreviations that you will frequently come across when talking or reading about data warehouse information. Technicians are the biggest culprits of rapidly inventing new mnemonics. In fact, many acronyms are reused or duplicated.[1] This glossary is like a decoder ring, which will come in handy throughout the life of the data warehouse project. It will be useful for future nondata warehouse projects as well. The business manager can use the glossary as a tool for future conversations and communications with information technologists.

Terms, Mnemonics, and Acronyms[2]

access   The procedure for creating, reading, updating, or deleting data on the physical storage unit holding the data for the data warehouse.

access method   A software technique used to transfer specific data from the hardware that contains it.

access path The road map that the software follows to retrieve data from a table/entity in the data warehouse.

ad hoc queries Unscheduled and possibly not predefined inquiries about the data warehouse. If not predefined, the inquiry usually occurs only once when the requester needs the data. If it is predefined, it could occur many times, or whenever the requester needs the data.

aggregation The process of combining several data values into a new data value (for example, the sum of all sale receipts).

alias An alternative name for a specific piece of physical data.

alternate key Another means other than the primary one to access a specific group or object of data. For example, to find a specific customer by the customer identifier, you would probably use a primary key. To find the same customer by customer name, you would probably use an alternate key.

application program interface (API) Application program interface (API) is a common set of parameters that is required for multiple programs to communicate. This is a common term when multiple software packages need to "link" or "pass" information between themselves.

architecture A model of the physical technological environment that supports the data warehouse. For more information about architecture, refer to Chapter 5, "How to Write a Winning Business Case."

artificial intelligence (AI) Artificial intelligence (AI) refers to computer applications that are capable of performing functions typically associated with human decision making. The most common examples are found with diagnosis type applications.

associative entity An object in the data model that ties multiple business entities. The purpose is to resolve a many-to-many relationship between two entities. For example, a customer may have multiple addresses and multiple customers who live at the same address. Part of the normalization process (analysis) is to develop an associative entity that contains the primary key from two or more other entities that require an association.

atomic Data stored in a decision support system or data warehouse.

attribute A property of an entity.

audit trail   Data about the activities of data, usually the update, creation, or deletion of specific pieces of data. Examples of audit trail data are usually a date and time stamp of when the change occurred and who changed the data.

availability   A metric used to evaluate a system's reliability. The value is usually presented in a percentage format of the difference between the agreed availability of the data warehouse and the actual availability to business users. It is sometimes referred to as "up time."

batch window   The scheduled unavailability of the data warehouse to business users. This time typically occurs daily or on weekends. This time is used to maintain the data warehouse and run scheduled, predefined reports that require no intervention by the business user. This time is typically scheduled during off-peak hours or hours the business community typically does not require direct access to the data warehouse.

buffer   An area of physical storage that holds data temporarily in main memory. Many buffers exist and are typically used while data is being transmitted, received, read, or written. Frequently requested data may also be contained in a buffer. This specific type of buffer is referred to as *cache*.

business events   An occurrence requiring activity within the data warehouse. Four types of business events can occur:

1. *Ad hoc.* An unscheduled request for data. What-if analysis usually falls into this category.

2. *Standard.* A predefined request for data. Before the board meets to discuss quarterly dividends, specific reports are run and distributed about the corporation's health.

3. *Conditional.* Request for data is a result of a condition being reached. For example, inventory falling below a comfort level causes a report of buying patterns.

4. *Time-initiated.* Request for data due to a point in time being reached. For example, end of month or year reporting.

business intelligence   As defined by the Gartner Group, business intelligence is the corporation's ability to access and explore information usually contained in a data warehouse. With the information the corporation can analyze and develop insights and understanding that lead to improved and informed business decision making. Examples of business intelligence tools are: decision support systems, executive information systems, and query- and report-writing tools.

business rules   The laws that the data, its relationships, and manipulation must satisfy. A distributor may purchase any number of a specific product. However, the distributor may only purchase one for demonstration that can not be resold. A vehicle may be sold multiple times but can only be sold as new once. These rules impact the organization of the data contained in the data warehouse.

capability maturity model (CMM)   A framework that demonstrates the key elements of an effective software process. The CMM describes an evolutionary improvement path for software development. It begins with an ad hoc, immature process and evolves into a mature, disciplined process, on a path layed out in five levels. The Software Engineering Institute (SEI) of Carnegie Mellon University devised the capability maturity model (CMM) for improving the software process.

capacity planning   The process of identifying the growth of the data warehouse and its impact on the technological architecture.

cardinality   The relationship of one business thing to another. For example, for every customer, there may be up to six telephone numbers. The average number will be two. Therefore, the cardinality would be represented as 0:N with the indication of 0:6/2, meaning that a customer may not have any telephone numbers. The customer could have up to six but most customers will only have two. The information technologist will discuss the cardinality values to predict the size of the data warehouse.

classification   It is the process of predicting future data results from historical patterns. Sometimes referred to as supervised learning. For more information on this technique, refer to Data Mining in Chapter 4, "What Do I Do With It Now?"

client   The receiver of data. Most commonly a personal computer.

clustering   A physically stored block of data.

column   A vertical table (or spreadsheet) containing values of the same type of information. A row crosses many columns.

component-based software development   A technique for developing and implementing software by business function. Often used with incremental development approaches.

computer-aided software engineering (CASE)   A graphical tool with intelligence used by the information technologist to assist in developing the data warehouse model.

computer-based training (CBT)   Software developed specifically for training data warehouse users.

contention   When multiple users or programs simultaneously attempt to access the exact same data.

critical success factors (CSFs)   The limited number of areas in which satisfactory results will ensure competitive performance for the individual, department, or organization. CSFs are the few key areas where "things must go right" for the business to flourish and the manager's goals to be attained. For data warehousing, business involvement, training, and executive sponsorship are a few critical success factors. It is important to identify the CSFs as early as possible in the project's life cycle. For more information on CSFs refer to Chapter 5, "How to Write a Winning Business Case."

data   The smallest unit of information.

data administrator (DA)   The role in the information technology organization responsible for identifying, documenting, and modeling the business data requirements. For more information about this role, refer to Chapter 7, "What to Do About Employee Training and Education."

data cleansing and scrubbing   The process of converting data from one source to another by passing it through a software filter to eliminate inconsistencies or invalid (such as redundant and inconsistent) information. Data cleansing and scrubbing include four manipulations of data from the source to the data warehouse.

1. Data cleaning includes manipulating data values to be consistent (for example, converting an abbreviation of "Rd." to the full word of Road or visa versa).

2. Missing values includes supplying a formula to calculate a value to be stored or to store a default value (for example, calculating an

average number of employees for a given month to be stored for a December total).

3. Data derivation values also include calculations. However, this process stores values that are based upon existing data. The data does not have to be stored as it can always be recalculated when needed. However, for performance reasons, it might prove valuable to store this "derived" data. Remember, the value is not at its base form (for example, storing a calculated ROI on a month-by-month basis).

4. Merging data values are the results of combining data from multiple databases and represents a specific, tailored view of data values already stored in the data warehouse. The merging data, however, may not be stored in the data warehouse but must be separate for the business manager's use.

For more information, please refer to Chapter 2, "How a Data Warehouse Is Built."

data dictionary   A software tool that contains information about the data, its relationships, formats, business meaning, location, etc.

data mapping   The activity of correlating data requirements to existing data.

data mart   A data mart is not mutually exclusive but a subset of a data warehouse. It is designed to support the unique business unit requirements of a specific application. Many information technology organizations are implementing distinct and separate data marts. Although this may seem beneficial to the corporation in the short term, the result may be several informational storage facilities that produce inconsistent data results whenever an executive requires information from multiple data marts. Therefore, a data mart implementation is beneficial when it satisfies specific needs of the business units. However, this process should be implemented based upon a data warehousing strategy to control consistency across data marts.

data mining   Ability to search through large pieces of information for answers to a business question. The search can be generic but the objective of the question must be measurable. Data mining is the process of discovering meaningful new correlations, patterns, and trends by sifting through large amounts of data stored within a data warehouse using pattern recognition technologies as well as statistical and mathematical techniques.

data model   An architectural view of the data, its relationships, and definitions.

data replication   The process of ensuring the consistency of data across multiple servers in a distributed environment.

data security   A means of protecting data in the data warehouse against unauthorized use, alteration, or deletion.

data storage   The physical media to hold the data.

data volatility   The frequency the value of the data changes.

data warehouse   A storage facility of informational-type data that is integrated, subject-oriented, time-based, and nonvolatile. It is designed to be easier to access than operational data and reduces contention for the data. The data contained in the data warehouse originated elsewhere either internal or external to the corporation. It is integrated and cleansed from various sources.

database   A collection of data values in an organized format defined by the physical data model.

database administrator (DBA)   A role responsible for defining, documenting, and maintaining the physical database. For more information about this role, refer to Chapter 7, "What to Do About Employee Training and Education."

database management system (DBMS)   Computer system software that manages the physical data.

deadlock   A condition reached when a request is made for data that is currently being used by someone who has sole access to it. This creates a serious performance problem.

decision support system (DSS)   Typically a "read-only" application designed to support managerial decision making.

denormalization   The technique usually done for performance reasons. It entails modifying the "normalized" data model to optimize it for the physical environment.

dense   When most of the joining points of all dimensions in the database or results contain data values. Although this is a matter of opinion, the percentage of data values should be more than 90 percent to be considered dense.

derived data   Data that is not stored in its base or lowest formats. It involves a calculation upon one or more pieces of data. For example, monthly summaries of sales activity could be stored in the data warehouse either with or without the individual components that made up the derived data.

dimension   A data attribute that is used as a structural construction for a multidimensional view, results, or database. An actual sales spreadsheet may have the column headings of months of the year. The rows represent all of the sales regions. Both the sales regions and months of the year are dimensions.

distributed databases   Databases that are geographically dispersed but are controlled by the same database management system (DBMS).

distribution model   A physical model that shows how function and data are distributed over a series of separate machines.

download   The transferring a copy of data from one device to another.

drill-down/up analysis   A technique of exploring the components of data. Drill-down analysis goes from summary to detailed information (for example, identifying the cause of a specific drop in sales for a specific product for a specific month). The opposite is drill-up analysis. Drill-up analysis starts with the detail and goes up to the summary to identify concepts or trends.

dumb terminal   A device whose sole purpose is to gather and display data. All processing is done remotely from the device.

electronic data interchange (EDI)   A means of communicating between corporations using a predefined electronic format. An example would be a money transfer system.

encoding   Physically storing an abbreviation for a data value (for example, *Rd* for road, *M* for Male).

encryption   The process of converting data from a recognizable form to an unrecognizable one for security reasons.

entity   A person, place, or thing that is of interest to the business, (for example, customer, product, or package).

entity relationship diagram   A data model that represents a wide business area. A precursor to the logical or business data model.

executive information systems (EIS):. A computer system designed to support drill-down or trend analysis for executives.

expert systems   A system that captures data and "learns" about human activities.

extranet   An Internet that crosses or joins multiple corporations. For example, multiple insurance companies may wish to share their claim histories to identify fraud. For more information on this topic, refer to the Internet in Chapter 4, "What Do I Do With It Now?"

facilitation   A meeting to resolve a specific set of objectives. The meeting is usually between attendees of different departments and led by an impartial leader.

facilitator   A person whose declared role is to guide a meeting toward its objective. The person is responsible for designing the meeting and carrying it out. The person is not responsible for the content of the discussion and the resulting products. The person is usually trained to be an impartial leader.

field   A data item. The term *field* can be used to represent an element in the database or an entry point for specific information on a computer screen.

foreign key   A primary key in one entity that is also contained in another entity to build a physical association between the two. The second entity contains the foreign key.

formula   A database object within a multidimensional database that defines the data relationships. It represents a calculation, rule, or other expression for manipulating data. Formulas define relationships among members.

graphical user interface (GUI)   A window-type display for supplying or displaying information retrieved from the data warehouse.

hit   A slang term for data that satisfies the search criteria.

homonyms   Identical names that refer to different attributes.

index   A means for identifying a specific group of data. The index consists of one or more data items. Sometimes referred to as a *key*.

influence analysis   The process of identifying the cause of results. For more information about this technique, refer to data mining in Chapter 4 "What Do I Do With It Now?"

infrastructure   The model that includes the technical architecture as well as the software to support the data warehouse. For more information about infrastructure, refer to Chapter 5, "How to Write a Winning Business Case."

instance   A single occurrence in an entity or a specific row in a table.

integrated services digital network (ISDN)   Telecommunication technology that enables the transfer of data and voice through the same telephone lines.

internet   An open access method for a wide range of information. For more information about this topic, refer to the Internet in Chapter 4 "What Do I Do With It Now?"

intranet   An Internet within a single corporation. For more information about this topic, refer to the Internet in Chapter 4, "What Do I Do With It Now?"

join   Concatenating or merging two separate groups or tables of data to satisfy an inquiry.

level of abstraction   Manipulation of the data to satisfy a specific dimension.

local area network (LAN)   The linking of multiple personal computers to a server.

metadata   Data about the data. It includes the attributes of and information about each piece of data that will be contained in the data warehouse, such as business definition, size, format, or location. Provides the context that transforms the warehouse data into meaningful business information.

middleware   Software from a third-party to be used with a data warehouse implementation using different technological platforms. The software is usually not provided by the hardware or database vendor. The software makes it possible to tie disparate systems together so that they function as one logical system. The business user, therefore, sees only one data warehouse system.

multidimensional arrays   A group of data arranged by the dimensions of the data. A single piece of data in a two-dimensional array is identified by row and column location. A simple example is a cell in a spreadsheet. Dimensions greater than two are feasible with data warehouses. Therefore, a specific piece of data could be the joining of any number of variables and dimensions such as time, products, percentages, and geographical location.

multidimensional databases (MDDB)   A view of the data that has more than two sides (dimensions) that are dependent upon one another. This is sometimes referred to as a *cube*.

network   The infrastructure to support telecommunications between two or more points.

neural networks   A multilayered network architecture that works with a data warehouse and "learns" how to solve a problem based on examples. First, the data is divided or sorted into groups or clusters according to rules coded in programs that are defined by the business knowledge experts. Then algorithms, defined by the business knowledge experts, are used to create predictive models that capture the nonlinear interactions between factors.

normalization   A technique of organizing the data into the purest representation of the business.

on-line analytical processing (OLAP)   A database designed to support analytical processing such as decision support. For more information, refer to Chapter 2, "How a Data Warehouse Is Built."

on-line transaction processing (OLTP)   A database designed to support transactional processing. For more information, refer to Chapter 2, "How a Data Warehouse Is Built."

operational data store (ODS)   A loosely used term to represent a real-time data warehouse that does not contain history and/or is used for operational, mission-critical purposes versus analysis and reporting purposes.

optimization   The process of denormalizing a normalized data model to take advantage of the technological environment.

parallel processing   The means of processing the same inquiry against partitioned databases.

partition   The segmentation of data across multiple storage mechanisms.

patterns   The common usage and access of data.

peak period   The time that the most usage of the data warehouse occurs.

platform   The technological piece such as hardware, database software, the operating system, and network software components that make up the physical layer of the data warehouse. The layer could be all the same or different for each communication point between the end user and the data warehouse.

populating   The process of extracting data from another source and storing it in the data warehouse according to the format and location defined by the data warehouse structure. The process includes extracting, transforming, consolidating, and cleansing the data from the original source before placing the data in its defined location in the data warehouse. For more information, refer to Chapter 2, "How A Data Warehouse Is Built."

primary key   The data item or group of data items that uniquely distinguishes one row in a table from another.

prototyping   The process of demonstrating a version of, but not the completed, data warehouse. The purpose is to obtain concurrence in understanding the final data warehouse. For more information on prototyping, refer to Chapter 2, "How a Data Warehouse Is Built."

referential integrity   A mechanism of the database management system to ensure that the deletion of data in one table is also done to related information. For example, if a customer is deleted, all addresses and telephone numbers related to the customer are also deleted. This ensures the validity of predefined relationships.

replication server   A hot backup for another server. It contains the same data and is available if the primary server becomes nonoperational.

repository The physical mechanism that holds the metadata information.

requirements engineering The process of eliciting, analyzing, documenting, verifying, managing, and approving requirements as they evolve from business ideas and become implemented solutions.

requirements management The defined process of controlling the different levels of requirements through the development cycle.

response time The amount of time between pressing the enter key and receiving a response.

return on investment (ROI) The difference between the tangible benefits and the tangible costs of a specific project. Executives use this percentage to decide if the project is worth the investment by the corporation, to guage the progress and continuance of the project, and measure the success of the project. For more information on ROI, refer to Chapter 5, "How to Write a Winning Business Case."

row A horizontal table (or spreadsheet) containing values of the same type of information. A column crosses many rows.

search engine The software facility on the Internet that receives inquiries for reading data contained in a data warehouse. For more information on this topic, refer to the Internet in Chapter 4, "What Do I Do With It Now?"

server Computer hardware that holds data or processes functions that support multiple hardware clients.

schema A representation of the data structure.

slice A subset of a multidimensional database, view, or results.

sparse When the majority of joining points of all dimensions in the a database or the results do not contain data values. Though this is a matter of opinion, the percentage of data values should be less than 40 percent to be considered sparse.

star schema The physical implementation of a data mart or warehouse that incorporates the distribution of data to multiple clients. The physical model or diagram of the implementation represents a star design. The difficulty of this type of implementation is the synchronization of the data being downloaded. For more information on data warehouse architecture and infrastructure, refer to Chapter 2, "How a Data Warehouse Is Built" and Chapter 5, "How to Write a Winning Business Case."

structured query language (SQL)   A data definition and manipulation language developed for relational database management systems such as those used for data warehousing.

subject database   A data warehouse dedicated to supporting data that is related to a specific business subject (for example, financial, customer service, or human resources).

subject matter expert   A person who has detailed knowledge of a specific business subject.

three-tier architecture   The technological environment that typically encompasses multiple technological platforms. The technological environment has a host that is usually a mainframe, a server that could be a WAN or LAN, and a personal computer or other workstation at the business manager's desk. For more information on three-tier architecture, refer to Chapter 2, "How A Data Warehouse Is Built."

three-tier reporting   Inquiries and reports are executed against a table of results that contains a subset of the data contained in the data warehouse. In other words, data is first extracted and formatted based upon an inquiry from the data warehouse. Additional queries and formatting are executed from the data extracted (table of results) from the first inquiry. This approach provides a performance enhancement if the business user wants to execute several "what-if" analyses against the same data. The business user would first create a "result's table" of a subset of the data warehouse data that will be used multiple times. The result's table is usually kept on his or her desktop and can be formatted (for example, aggregation of detail sales data into monthly values) to meet the specific needs of the business user. The what-if analysis would be executed against the result's table.

two-tier architecture   The technological environment that encompasses two points. At one point would be a server that may or may not be a mainframe. At the other point is a personal computer or other workstation at the business manager's desk. For more information on two-tier architecture, refer to Chapter 2, "How A Data Warehouse is Built."

two-tier reporting   Inquiries and reporting are executed directly against the data warehouse. One inquiry, one result. No additional inquiries are executed against the results.

trend analysis   The process for looking for patterns in the data over a period of time. For more information on this technique, refer to data mining in Chapter 4, "What Do I Do With It Now?"

uniform resource locator (URL)   The Internet address pointing to a specific web sight.

use cases   Another term for events. Encompasses business and physical events, such as the act of dropping down a menu selection on a computer screen.

user   The eventual user of the data warehouse.

very large database (VLDB)   For more information, refer to Chapter 5, "How to Write a Winning Business Case."

virtual data warehouse (VDW)   A concept developed by product vendors and consultants. The idea is that you do not have to create a separate storage facility to be a data warehouse. Instead, with improved technology, the data can remain where it is in operational storage facilities. Tools like data mining would work directly with the operational data. The key issues with this approach are data integrity and the response time impact on transactional processing.

visualization   A tool that provides a graphical presentation of the results of specific inquiry to the data. Pie and bar charts represent two-dimensional visualization. Three-dimensional views are typically seen in architectural or engineering environments. Visualization represents real-time depiction of multidimensional data.

wide area network (WAN)   The linking of multiple networks that are not located in the same geographical location.

world wide web (WWW)   The Internet.

Summary

This glossary contains commonly used terms and mnemonics to be used when discussing or reading about data warehousing or whenever conversations occur between business representatives and information technologists. The definitions use nontechnical terminology to assist the reader in understanding the topic of data warehousing. When more information is needed by the Business Manager to obtain an in-depth understanding of the terms, references are made to the appropriate chapters in this book.

Notes

Preface

1. Some business organizations refer to this role as the "subject matter expert" or SME. It is the person who best understands a specific business subject.

Chapter 1

1. Internet, for the purposes of this book, is generic for Internet (which anyone has the opportunity to access either for free or for a fee), Intranet (access to the information is internal to a particular organization), and Extranet (internal within specific but multiple organizations, such as only between insurance companies).

2. For more information on interfacing data warehouses with other technologies, refer to Chapter 4, "What Do I Do With It Now?"

3. Data mining is a tool that works in conjunction with a data warehouse. It "mines" or searches and analyzes the data warehouse to uncover patterns and relationships. It applies advanced statistical analysis and modeling techniques to raw data. Data mining assists the business user in the knowledge-discovery process. Data mining will be discussed further in Chapter 4, "What Do I Do With It Now?"

4. The actual figures applied to tangible benefits and costs are discussed in Chapter 5, "How to Write a Winning Business Case." The purpose of

this section is to introduce the benefits and costs associated with building a data warehouse to develop a level of understanding of what it is.

5. Throughout this book, specific success stories are provided to illustrate the value data warehouse implementation has on a corporation.

6. Single place does not imply a single physical place, but rather a single source of information. More about the physical place will be discussed in the section on how a data warehouse is built.

7. Cleansing the data is a term used to convert data contained in legacy systems into what is considered more useful or accurate format. An example of cleansing the data is converting any abbreviations that may incorrectly imply multiple records of the same item. For example, Mr. E. Smith, Mr. Edwin Smith, Ed Smith are the same individual listed in separate records as three individuals.

8. As defined by the OLAP council, on-line analytical processing is "a category of software technology that enables analysts, managers, and executives to gain insight into data through fast, consistent, interactive access to a wide variety of possible views of information that has been transformed from raw data to reflect the real dimensionally of the enterprise as understood by the user." William Inmon, *Managing the Data Warehouse* (New York: Wiley, 1996).

9. A data warehouse provides information. It is the responsibility of the user of the information to gain knowledge from it. This is an important point made by Dr. Edward Demings. Information is not knowledge!

10. Concept developed by Peter Senge.

11. Having a data warehouse in place does not guarantee that the data is accurate. Establishing accuracy is part of the cleansing process discussed in Chapter 2, "How a Data Warehouse Is Built." Having the data in a single source allows everyone to view the same information, thus minimizing multiple interpretations.

12. Notice that data warehousing is not limited to a bi-dimensional view of the data. Tools exist when working with data warehouses that provide multidimensional views of data. These tools are described in more detail in Chapter 4, "What Do I Do With It Now?"

13. Knowledge management is a broad term defined by GIGA (Connie Moore) that encompasses an organization's work processes, best practices, information technology infrastructure, and business culture for acquiring, retaining, updating, sharing, and reusing actionable, meaningful information that is gathered systematically on an ongoing basis.

14. Data mining is a term used for a tool that works specifically for statistical analysis of detailed data contained in a data warehouse. This tool is discussed in detail in Chapter 4, "What Do I Do With It Now?"

15. The META Group is one of three research organizations recommended by this book for more information on data warehousing. For more information, see Chapter 7, "What to Do About Employee Training and Education."

16. Http://www.metagroup.com Trends: Application Delivery Strategies, July 11, 1997.

17. IBM Business Intelligence Solutions Symposium held May 5, 1998, at Madison Square Garden in New York City.

18. Several years ago, a home shopping retailer increased its handling charges by $0.25. This had no effect on the customer base but significantly increased revenue.

19. Http://www.dw-institute.com/cases/energy.htm.

20. Deregulation powers Entergy's award-winning data warehouse: Http://www.dw-institute.com/cases/energy.htm. Page 3 of 3.

21. For more information on interfacing data warehouse with other technologies, refer to Chapter 4, "What Do I Do With It Now?"

22. This is not to imply that it will take a few years to derive benefits from a data warehouse. Chapter 2, "How a Data Warehouse Is Built," discusses alternative implementation approaches that provide incremental benefits to the business community.

Chapter 2

1. For more information on building a business case for data warehousing, refer to Chapter 5, "How to Write a Winning Business Case."

2. Refer to the Appendix for a more detailed description of the activities involved in developing a data warehouse.

3. This process is described in more detail in Chapter 3, "Keys to a Successful Implementation," because it is the most important cause for success or failure when implementing a data warehouse of any size.

4. Examples of how to discuss and present your request to a manager are discussed in Chapter 5, "How to Write a Winning Business Case."

5. This process is discussed in greater detail in Chapter 5, "How to Write a Winning Business Case."

6. CitySPIn User Conference presentation by Dr. Howard Rubin, September 2, 1997.

7. Dimension refers to adding an additional access with which to view information. For example, a business user may wish to view sales not only by region and month but also by product.

8. Populating is a term for feeding the data warehouse with data values from the identified source files or data structures.

9. Requirements are approximately half the reason for failed implementation of any technological solution. Therefore, a discussion of good requirements is contained in Chapter 3, "Keys to a Successful Implementation."

10. "Challenges Faced by the Data Warehousing Pioneers," *The Data Warehouse Institute Flash Report,* June, 1997.

11. Infrastructure and architecture are discussed in more detail in Chapter 5, "How to Write a Winning Business Case."

12. A business model is sometimes referred to by technicians as a "logical" model.

13. A four-tier architecture is discussed to represent the Internet's access to a three-tier data warehouse.

14. For more detailed technical information on data replication, see *Data Replication: Tools & Techniques for Managing Distributed Information,* by Marie Buretta.

15. Applications can also be partitioned. Functionality of an application is separated or partitioned into tiers of the architecture in the same manner as the data.

16. Keep in mind that some users will require basic personal computer training. Therefore, make certain that such a course is available in your organization.

17. Reasons are described in detail in Chapter 3, "Keys to a Successful Implementation."

18. Data mining is discussed in more detail in Chapter 4, "What Do I Do With It Now?"

Chapter 3

1. This chapter includes contributions from Burt Rosner who is a senior consultant with Spectrum Technologies.

2. When additional requirements are added to the scope of the project without eliminating other requirements or extending the delivery schedule, it is referred to as "scope creep." Manage the addition of requirements by evaluating each requirement against the business objectives. Determine if the increased work and new delivery schedule is worth the negative effect it may have on the ROI.

3. Figure 3-1 is derived from the IEEE's *Recommended Practice for Software Requirements Specifications,* IEEE standard 830-1993, pp. 5–8.

4. This process was defined by the shuttle project in *The Capability Maturity Model: Guidelines for Improving the Software Process,* by Mark C. Paulk, Charles V. Weber, Bill Curtis, Mary Beth Chrissis (Reading, Mass.: Addison-Wesley, 1995), pp. 103–105.

5. The figure is derived from the *IEEE Recommended Practice for Software Requirements Specifications,* IEEE standard 830–1993, p. 11.

6. Requirements engineering is a maturing discipline. New approaches to eliciting requirements are being studied and used throughout the academic, scientific, and business fields.

7. There are a number of different structured approaches used to bring people together and elicit information from them. The acronym JAD is used to represent all of them.

8. The executive sponsor should select the interviewees.

9. Derived requirements are requirements that evolve from the previous level of requirements. In this example, the derived requirements are more detailed than the original business requirements. Additional business requirements may be uncovered from the JAD sessions. These must be reviewed to determine if they should be considered part of the project when the scope is expanded.

10. For the purpose of data warehousing, quality represents the cohesion of many disciplines.

11. For more information about the maintenance process, refer to Chapter 2, "How a Data Warehouse Is Built," specifically, step seven of the eight-step process.

Chapter 4

1. Developing a successful business case is covered in two chapters. Chapter 5, "How to Write a Winning Business Case," discusses the gathering of the details. Chapter 6, "Selling the Business Case," discusses the process of convincing executive management.

2. For more information on the steps to building a data warehouse, refer to Chapter 2, "How a Data Warehouse Is Built."

3. This is a medium- to large-size data warehouse. Five hundred gigabytes is equivalent to approximately 500,000,000,000 bytes of storage, which is equivalent to approximately 500 personal computer disks. For more information on sizing a data warehouse, refer to Chapter 5, "How To Write a Winning Business Case."

4. Tools for the analysis, design, development, and implementation of a data warehouse should be chosen by technicians. Information on these types of tools is available in specialized technical periodicals and books written for the information technology community.

5. For more information on data warehouse infrastructure and its impact on growth, refer to Chapter 5, "How to Write a Winning Business Case."

6. For more information on success techniques for a data warehouse, refer to Chapter 3, "Keys to a Successful Implementation."

7. Brio Technology is located on the Internet at www.brio.com.

8. For more information on tiered architecture, refer to Chapter 2, "How a Data Warehouse Is Built."

9. For more information on tiered architecture, refer to Chapter 2, "How a Data Warehouse Is Built."

10. New enhancements to data warehouse software engines allow Excel spreadsheets to feed directly into the data warehouse.

11. Web queries are an additional feature of Excel 97, which can enhance the use of Internet and data warehouse technologies.

Chapter 5

1. For more information about reasons for data warehouse failures, see Chapter 3, "Keys to a Successful Implementation."

2. Corporations are willing to invest in major technological solutions, such as data warehouses, only if the gain from implementation will be significant marketplace infiltration, an opportunity to springboard ahead of competition, or the maintenance of its current status in the industry. If the competition is using a data warehouse that is affecting a corporation's bottom line, then the corporation will be required to follow suit just to survive. A business case must take this tone to reach the core of executive management's philosophy.

3. Until the year 2002, information technology organizations around the world will be mostly concerned with converting their current production systems to support the new century. Adding to that concern is the European Monetary Unit (EMU), which also falls into that time schedule. Your business case will have to be written to compete with both major tasks.

4. Information technology organizations have a history of building systems that do not meet the requirements of the business. These, in turn, result in "runaway" projects that have both cost and schedule overruns. One of the many mechanisms for maintaining control of a project is a business case. It is the first document produced in the development process. It immediately appoints the business area as the lead sponsor and controller of the project. It documents check-points for which information technology will be held accountable.

5. If possible, avoid sending this memo through the company's electronic mail facility. Many managers delete their e-mail without reading it. If you must use e-mail, send the message with a return receipt. Once you receive confirmation that the note was received and opened, follow up, in person, with a question that diplomatically confirms whether or not the manager read the electronic mail.

6. Every manager has his or her preferred style of receiving information. Make sure the format of this memo and its delivery matches your manager's and not yours.

7. The information technology contact is usually a project leader or manager who is responsible for the information technology projects of a specific business unit.

8. The term "charge back" refers to allocating every employee's or consultant's time to specific business units. Therefore, the business unit is paying for the individual at a corporate guideline rate.

9. An overview of different information technology organizations is provided in Chapter 7, "What to Do About Employee Training and Education."

10. Some organizations may have the data role split into several specialized areas: data architect, data analyst, and database analyst. The data architect is responsible for organizing global information. The data analyst may only be responsible for project level organization of information. The database analyst is responsible for the physical implementation and maintenance of information. The data security analyst is responsible for controlling access to information. The data planner is responsible for anticipating the equipment needed to support current and future growth of the amount of information to be kept. For smaller organizations, one individual may perform some or all of these roles. In even smaller organizations, the data analyst, the business analyst, and the requirements engineer may be one and the same individual. However, for this particular scenario, the most common role is that of data analyst. The data analyst's role and responsibilities are described in more detail in Chapter 7, "What to Do About Employee Training and Education."

11. "Cleanse the data" is an expression used by data analysts for correcting, reformatting, and standardizing information contained in existing files. For example, one customer may be listed multiple times with multiple customer numbers in the data files (for example, once as Mr. E. Smith and another time as Mr. Edwin Smith). Another concern is multiple addresses. Some files have *street* spelled out while others have it abbreviated. Tools do exist to assist in cleansing the data. However, it is still a very time-consuming task.

12. If you are having difficulty in identifying tangible benefits, contact someone within your organization's financial department. They have the skills to identify the cost-savings to anything and would enjoy the opportunity to be part of a project from the beginning.

13. Each of these areas will be able to provide a dollar value to having critical performance statistics at their fingertips.

14. For more detailed information on how to define scope, see Chapter 2, "How a Data Warehouse Is Built."

15. See Chapter 7, "What to Do About Employee Training and Education," for a sampling of vendors and industry specialists.

16. For more information about writing good business requirements, refer to Chapter 3, "Keys to a Successful Implementation."

17. For the first implementation phase, try to use as much existing hardware, network, and software as possible. This economy will enhance your chances of obtaining the appropriate resources and funding by minimizing cost during the proof-of-concept stage.

18. This process is called "cleansing the data." For more information, see Chapter 2, "How a Data Warehouse Is Built."

19. Today, hardware costs aggressively change over shorter periods of time. Therefore, use an average cost for any piece of equipment.

20. Some of the information conained in the data warehouse will be compressed. However, for this estimate, uncompressed data should anticipate any replication of information due to unanticipated growth.

21. For every successful data warehouse implementation, there are hordes of new uses and users who want to use this information. For

more information on anticipating growth, see Chapter 4, "What Do I Do With It Now?"

22. People who find the data warehouse difficult to use will not use the product. Nonuse of the product is an unsuccessful data warehouse implementation. Therefore, forget any future funding or additional resources. The project will be considered a failure.

23. This is true unless the user is the chairman of the board, chief executive officer, or other high ranking executive.

24. If possible, leave new network locations for future implementation phases. After a first successful implementation, future budget will be easier to obtain.

25. Data cleansing is the biggest tangible benefit to the organization. However, it must be explained carefully. Provide specific instances of information conflicts that affect analysis.

26. Platinum Technology/LBMS/Process Engineer has a data warehouse template that assists information technologists in determining development effort. It also includes a proven development template for implementing a data warehouse.

27. Do not try to cut costs by hiring low cost technologists or by eliminating tasks from the development plan. Building a data warehouse is a risky investment. Get the most for your dollars by using individuals with experience in data warehousing. Remember, it is better to pay the price up front than paying the price for a shoddy end product.

28. Curt Hall, *Data Mining: Tools & Reviews* (Arlington, Mass.: Cutter Information Corp.).

29. A defect is anything that does not meet the business user's expectation.

Chapter 6

1. Tangible goals carry more weight than intangible ones. It is easier for decision makers to quickly identify the ROI.

2. For more information about the key information technology players in your organization, refer to Chapter 7, "What to Do About Employee Training and Education."

3. For more information about writing quality requirements, refer to Chapter 3, "Keys to a Successful Implementation."

4. W. Edwards Deming was a leading quality expert. One of his many contributions to quality was this simple four-step process.

5. Make this very clear to the decision makers. All you are guaranteeing is the first estimate for the first milestone, not the implementation of the entire data warehouse.

6. I have never seen one major project or major enhancement reach implementation without at least one unforeseen event occurring to impact the project. This list contains the most common that I have witnessed throughout my career.

7. This particular risk carries a double-edged sword. It is important to make information technologists aware of the business implications of delays. However, be very careful with the countermeasure. A countermeasure cannot be to reduce analysis, design, or testing time since it will sacrifice quality and increase the chance of project failure. Adding more programmers to a project already behind schedule just makes the project later. Therefore, a countermeasure for this type of project should be that proper management and estimating techniques are used to determine a realistic schedule. Make certain that business will support information technology during each phase of the development cycle.

8. All mission-critical applications hopefully will be updated by the Year 2000. The two years that follow will be spent upgrading all other remaining systems, files, and repairing defects.

9. It has been the experience of the author that this occurs in approximately one out of every four projects that uses this business case format.

10. Tzu Sun, *Art of War* (New York: Oxford University Press, 1988). Never fight a battle when you can have someone else fight it for you!

Chapter 7

1. The author of this book is currently one of the many data warehousing experts who is a member of this organization.

2. LBMS was recently purchased by Platinum Technology, a subsidiary of the company, and has the same level of superb support.

3. Remember, these books (and this book in particular) were selected as good sources for the nontechnical person. IDEF1X is a notation for data diagrams that is used by the government and is becoming a standard in the business industry as well. Do not let the name of this specific book intimidate you.

4. Remember, some users will require basic personal computer usage or spreadsheet training.

5. Uniform Resource Locator (an address for a specific web site).

6. Requirements engineering is a new role that is evolving in many information technology organizations. They may have some of the responsibilities that a data or business analyst currently holds when interfacing with the business community.

7. Business process restrictions may be considered business rules.

8. It is the personal belief of the author that data warehouse consultants have domain knowledge of requirements engineering. They must understand the concepts of a data warehouse and how it must be used. The author has found that having an extensive knowledge in the business domain has prevented many consultants from listening to the needs of the business. Therefore, the consultants tend to implement a filtered view of the requirements. When selecting a consultant, put a higher priority on requirements engineering for data warehouse solutions than on the amount of knowledge of your business. No consultant has detailed business requirement knowledge as strong as yours!

Appendix

1. Refer to Chapter 7, "What To Do About Employee Training and Education," for sources for data warehouse project work breakdown structure templates.

2. This template has been customized from a base data warehouse process template supplied by Platinum Technology/LBMS, which is a company that specializes in software development process templates. Its template comes complete with activities and task descriptions, inputs and outputs, dependencies as well as roles and responsibilities. For more information about Platinum Technology/LBMS and its product, refer to its web site (www.platinum.com).

3. RFI/RFP is the abbreviation for request for information or request for proposal. It encompasses a list of your selection criteria as to what the tool must do or support in order to evaluate it. When possible, obtain a demonstration copy of the tool for at least 3 months of evaluation.

4. Refer to Chapter 5, "Writing a Winning Business Case," for guidelines about developing a data warehouse business case.

5. Refer to Chapter 6, "Selling a Winning Business Case," for guidelines about presenting a data warehouse business case.

Technophobia Avoidance Glossary

1. For example, ISA in the personal computer world represents industry standard architecture. For data warehousing, ISA represents information system architecture. Similarly, SDLC in the telecommunications world refers to synchronous data link control. For software development, SDLC stands for software development life cycle. For simplicity's sake, only the data warehouse terms and references will be listed.

2. ACRONYM is an acronym unto itself. It represents: **A**bbreviated **C**oded **R**endition **O**f **N**ame **Y**ielding **M**eaning. Refer to web site, www.ucc.ie/acronyms/, for additional acronyms not contained in this glossary.

Bibliography

Books

Adriaans, Pieter, et al. *Data Mining.* Reading, Mass.: Addison-Wesley, 1996.

Anahory, Sam, and Dennis Murray. *Data Warehousing in the Real World.* Reading, Mass.: Addison-Wesley, 1997.

Berry, Michael J. A., and Gordon Linoff. *Data Mining Techniques: For Marketing, Sales, and Customer Support.* New York: John Wiley & Sons, 1997.

Bigus, Joseph P. *Data Mining With Neural Networks: Solving Business Problems from Application Development to Decision Support.* New York: McGraw-Hill, 1996.

Bouldin, Barbara M. *Agents of Change: Managing the Introduction of Automated Tools.* Englewood Cliffs, N.J.: Yourdon Press, 1989.

Brooks, Frederick P. *The Mythical Man-Month: Essays on Software Engineering, Anniversary Edition.* Reading, Mass.: Addison-Wesley, 1995.

Bruce, Thomas A. *Designing Quality Databases With IDEF1X Information Models.* New York: Dorset House Publishing, 1992.

Buretta, Marie. *Data Replication: Tools & Techniques for Managing Distributed Information.* New York: John Wiley & Sons, 1997.

Cabena, Pater, et al. *Discovering Data Mining From Concept to Implementation.* Englewood Cliffs, N.J.: Prentice-Hall, 1997.

Devlin, Barry. *Data Warehouse: From Architecture to Implementation.* Reading, Mass.: Addison Wesley Longman, 1997.

Dhar, Vasant, and Roger Stein. *Seven Methods for Transforming Corporate Data into Business Intelligence.* Englewood Cliffs, N.J.: Prentice-Hall, 1997.

Fayyad, Usama M., et al. *Advances in Knowledge Discovery and Data Mining.* Boston: MIT Press, 1996.

Flavin, Matt. *Fundamental Concepts of Information Modeling.* Englewood Cliffs, N.J.: Yourdon Press, 1981.

Gause, Donald C., and Gerald M. Weinberg. *Are Your Lights On?* New York: Dorset House, 1990.

———. *Exploring Requirements: Quality Before Design.* New York: Dorset House Publishing, 1989.

Groth, Robert. *Data Mining: A Hands-On for Business Professionals.* Englewood Cliffs, N.J.: Prentice-Hall, 1998.

Hackney, Douglas. *The Seven Deadly Sins of Data Warehousing.* Reading, Mass.: Addison-Wesley, 1998.

———. *Understanding and Implementing Successful Data Marts.* Reading, Mass.: Addison-Wesley, 1997.

Haisten, Michael. *Planning a Data Warehouse Project.* Vital Technologies (a consulting company).

Hay, David C. *Data Model Patterns: Conventions of Thought.* New York: Dorset House, 1996.

Humphrey, Watts S. *A Discipline for Software Engineering.* Reading, Mass.: Addison-Wesley, 1995.

———. *Managing the Software Process.* Reading, Mass.: Addison-Wesley, 1989.

Inmon, W.H. *Building the Data Warehouse,* 2nd ed., New York: John Wiley & Sons, 1996.

———. *Practical Techniques for Building Dimensional Data Warehouses.* New York: John Wiley & Sons, 1996.

———. *Using the Data Warehouse.* New York: John Wiley & Sons, 1994.

Inmon, W.H., et al. *Managing the Data Warehouse: Practical Techniques.* New York: John Wiley & Sons, 1997.

Kennedy, Ruby L., et al. *Solving Data Mining Problems Through Pattern Recognition,* Data Warehousing Institute Series. Englewood Cliffs, N.J.: Prentice-Hall, 1997.

Mattison, Rob. *Data Warehousing: Strategies, Technologies and Techniques.* New York: McGraw-Hill, 1996.

Paulk, Mark C., et al. *The Capability Maturity Model: Guidelines for Improving the Software Process.* Reading, Mass.: Addison-Wesley, 1995.

Poe, Vidette. *Building A Data Warehouse for Decision Support.* Englewood Cliffs, N.J.: Prentice-Hall, 1996.

Robertson, Susan, and James Robertson. *Complete Systems Analysis.* New York: Dorset House, 1996.

Schulmeyer, Gordon G., and James I. McManus. *Total Quality Management for Software.* New York: Van Nostrand Reinhold, 1992.

Simon, Alan. R. *Data Warehousing for Dummies.* San Mateo, Calif.: IDG Books Worldwide, 1997.

Tanler, Rick. *The Intranet Data Warehouse.* New York: John Wiley & Sons, 1997.

Weiss, Sholom M., and Nitia Indurkhya. *Predictive Data Mining: A Practical Guide.* Silicon Valley, Calif.: Morgan Kaufman Publishers, 1997.

Periodicals and Papers

Bischoff, Joyce. "Achieving Warehouse Success: DB2 Data Warehouse Architecture." *Database Programming & Design,* July 1994, pp. 27–28.

Block, J. "The Data Warehouse: From Operational To Information." *InSide Gartner Group This Week,* November 16, 1994.

Brethenoux, E., et al. "Data Warehouse, Data Mining, and Business Intelligence: The Hype Stops Here." *Strategic Analysis Report,* October 28, 1996.

Brogan, Bob. "The Data Warehouse and Privacy." *Journal of Data Warehousing,* Vol. 2, No. 2, April 1997, pp. 17–20.

Cataldo, Joseph. "Care & Feeding of the Data Warehouse." *Database Programming & Design,* December 1997, pp. 36–42.

Data Warehouse Institute. "The 1996 Summary of Roles & Responsibilities of Data Warehousing Professionals."

———. "1997 Fall Implementation Conference."

———. "Challenges Faced by the Data Warehousing Pioneers," flash report, June 1997.

David, M. "Multimedia Databases." *Database Programming & Design,* May 1997, pp. 26–35.

Eckerson, Wayne W. "Web-Based Query Tools and Architectures." *Journal of Data Warehousing,* Vol. 2, No. 2, April 1997.

Edelstein, Herb. "Exploiting the Hidden Trends in Your Data." *DB2 Magazine,* Spring 1997.

———. "Where the Data Mining Gold Rush Is Headed." *Database Programming & Design,* December 1996, pp. 78–80.

Glassey-Edholm, Katerine, Executive Vice President, Brio Technology. "Keys to the Data Warehouse: The Role Of Query Tools in Successful Data Warehouses," www.brio.com.

Gotthard, William, et al. "Mining Text Data." *DB2 Magazine,* December 1996, pp. 44–48.

Gray, Paul. "New Developments in Data Warehousing." *Journal of Data Warehousing,* Vol. 2, November 2, 1997, pp. 2–4.

Guderian, Dave, et al. "Keeping the Data Warehouse On Track.." *Database Programming & Design,* Vol. 11, No. 1, January 1997, pp. 39–47.

Haisten, Michael. "A History of Access and Analysis Tools." *Journal of Data Warehousing,* Vol. 1, No. 1, July 1996, pp. 46–60.

Hall, Curt. "Data Mining: Tools and Reviews." *Data Management Strategies,* January 1997.

———. "Data Mart Roundup." *Data Management Strategies,* August 1997.

———. "Data Warehousing: Architectures, Options, Issues, & Products," parts I, II & III. *Data Management Strategies,* February and March 1997.

———. "Trends." *Data Management Strategies,* April 1998.

Hanlon, Judith. "Data Warehousing in the Telecommunications Industry." *Journal of Data Warehousing,* Vol. 1, No. 1, July 1996, pp. 32–35.

Hill, Robert L. "The Right Stuff." *Database Programming & Design,* The Data Warehouse Special Edition, August, 1997.

IEEE Computer Society, Software Engineering Standards Committee. "IEEE Recommended Practice for Software Requirements Specifications." IEEE Std 830-1993.

Linoff, Gordon. "It's a Customer-Centric World." *Database Programming & Design,* Vol. 10, No. 13, December 1997.

Levin, Ellen J. "Data Warehousing in the Government Sector." *Journal of Data Warehousing,* Vol. 1, No. 1, July 1996, pp. 14–22.

Love, Bruce. "Strategic DSS/Data Warehouse: A Case Study In Failure." *Journal of Data Warehousing,* Vol. 1, No. 1, July 1996, pp. 36–40.

McFadden, Fred R., and Hugh J. Watson. "The World of Data Warehousing: Issues and Opportunities." *Journal of Data Warehousing,* Vol. 1, No. 1, July 1996, pp. 61–71.

Mena, Jesus. "Data Mining from the Ground Up." *Database Programming & Design,* Vol. 10, No. 2, February 1997, pp. 63–67.

Menninger, Dave. "And Now, Introducing the Data Warehouse." *Database Programming & Design,* Vol. 12, No. 11, November 1994, pp. 126–129.

Moriarty, Terry. "A Metadata Management How-To." *Database Programming & Design,* Vol. 10, No. 2, February 1997, pp.57–60.

Noaman, Amin Y. "Distributed Data Warehouse Architectures." *Journal of Data Warehousing,* Vol. 2, No. 2, April 1997, pp. 37–50.

Paller, Alan. "A Road Map for Data Warehousing." *Journal of Data Warehousing,* Vol. 1, No. 1, July 1996, pp. 7–13.

———. "Six Trends You Should Be Aware of: Data Warehousing Today." *Journal of Data Warehousing,* Vol. 1, No. 1, July 1996, pp. 41–45.

Park, Yong-Tae. "Strategic Uses of Data Warehouses: An Organization's Suitability for Data Warehousing." *Journal of Data Warehousing,* Vol. 2, No. 1, January 1997, pp. 24–33.

Parsaye, Kamran. "OLAP & Data Mining: Bridging the Gap." *Database Programming & Design*, Vol. 10, No. 2, February 1997, pp. 30–37.

Pascarella, Perry. "Harnessing Knowledge." *Management Review*, October 1997, pp. 37–40.

Rubin, Dr. Howard A. "Information Technology, Business Value & Software Development: Aligning IT Performance for Business Performance." Presentation at the September, 1997 CitySPIn User Meeting.

Simon, Alan R. "Making Sense of ODS." *Database Programming & Design*, Vol. 11, No. 6, June 1998.

———. "The Watchful Enterprise." *Database Programming & Design*, Vol. 10, No. 13, December 1997, p. 26.

Skeels, David W. "Retail Wars: A Data Warehouse Can Be A Powerful Weapon." *Journal of Data Warehousing*, Vol. 1, No. 1, July 1996, pp. 23–31.

Sokol, Marc. *The Next Generation of Data Warehousing*. Computer Associates (a software company).

Stackowiak, Robert. "Why Bad Data Warehouses Happen To Good People." *Journal of Data Warehousing*, Vol. 2, No. 2, April 1997, pp. 33–36.

Thomann, Dr. James, and David L. Wells. "Real World Objects in the Data Warehouse: The Vision." *Journal of Data Warehousing*, Vol, 2, No. 2, April 1997, pp. 62–65.

Thomsen, Erik. "Dimensional Modeling: An Analytical Approach." *Database Programming & Design*, March 1997, pp. 29–35.

———. "Mining Your Way to OLAP." *Database Programming & Design*, September 1997, pp. 101–103.

———. "I Shop, Therefore I Am." *Database Programming & Design*, October 1997, pp. 78–80.

———Thomsen, Erik. "Where's the Glue?" *Database Programming & Design*, January 1998, pp. 75–76.

Wingfield, Teresa. "What are some key issues to consider when evaluating a data warehouse consultant for business requirements?" www.gigaweb.com, August 8, 1997. Document Number CQ.959293-TW97.

Winter, Richard. "A Strategy for Managing the Risk in Large Scale Data Warehouse Projects: An Application-Driven Approach." *Database Programming & Design,* Vol. 10, No. 2, February 1997, pp. 23–27.

Zackman, John. *An Information Systems Architecture Framework.* Guide Publication GPP-237, 1989.

Web Site Information

Acta Technology: www.acta.com

Brio Technology: www.brio.com

Data Warehouse Institute: www.dw-institute.com.

Gartner Group: www.gartner.com.

GIGA Information Group: www.gigaweb.com.

IBM: www.software.ibm.com/data.

IEEE (Transactions on Knowledge and Data Engineering): www.IEEE.org

Meta Group: www.meta.com.

NCR: www.ncr.com.

Online Analytical Processing Web Page: http://www.kenan.com/acu-mate/olaptrms.htm#array

Oracle: www.oracle.com

Platinum Technology: www.platinum.com

Sybase: www.sybase.com

Miscellaneous

LBMS Data Warehouse Process delivered with the Process Library, Version 7.0.

CITYSPIn User Conference presentation by Dr. Howard Rubin, September 2, 1997.

Index